T0260929

O'REILLY®
Strata
Making Data Work

Learn how to turn data into decisions.

From startups to the Fortune 500, smart companies are betting on data-driven insight, seizing the opportunities that are emerging from the convergence of four powerful trends:

- New methods of collecting, managing, and analyzing data

- Cloud computing that offers inexpensive storage and flexible, on-demand computing power for massive data sets

- Visualization techniques that turn complex data into images that tell a compelling story

- Tools that make the power of data available to anyone

Get control over big data and turn it into insight with O'Reilly's Strata offerings. Find the inspiration and information to create new products or revive existing ones, understand customer behavior, and get the data edge.

O'REILLY®

Visit oreilly.com/data to learn more.

Getting Started with Couchbase Server

MC Brown

O'REILLY®

Beijing · Cambridge · Farnham · Köln · Sebastopol · Tokyo

Getting Started with Couchbase Server

by MC Brown

Copyright © 2012 Couchbase, Inc. All rights reserved.
Printed in the United States of America.

Published by O'Reilly Media, Inc., 1005 Gravenstein Highway North, Sebastopol, CA 95472.

O'Reilly books may be purchased for educational, business, or sales promotional use. Online editions are also available for most titles (*http://my.safaribooksonline.com*). For more information, contact our corporate/institutional sales department: 800-998-9938 or *corporate@oreilly.com*.

Editors: Mike Loukides and Meghan Blanchette
Production Editor: Kristen Borg
Proofreader: O'Reilly Production Services

Cover Designer: Karen Montgomery
Interior Designer: David Futato
Illustrator: Robert Romano

Revision History for the First Edition:
   2012-06-08   First release
See *http://oreilly.com/catalog/errata.csp?isbn=9781449331061* for release details.

ISBN: 978-1-449-33106-1

[LSI]

1339082106

Table of Contents

Preface

Introduction

You've just launched your new web application, and by happy accident, it's gone viral and your usage has exploded from the few thousand users you originally expected to hundreds of thousands. If you are lucky, it will expand to millions within a few days.

If you are lucky, you designed your application with flexibility and expandability in mind. Depending on what environment you've chosen, you may have had to plan for a replication environment, using masters and slaves, or an application environment that allowed you to write to a central database, while reading from one of the replicated servers to aid performance.

With a little further planning, you may have decided to employ some kind of caching layer that allows you to store information in the RAM of your servers so that you don't have to make so many queries to the database for information that hasn't changed.

Surely there's an easier way?

Couchbase Server addresses many of these problems. It has a caching layer built in, and a built-in distribution system that doesn't require changes to your application. You can also expand your database system on the fly, without taking your application down, changing the configuration, or restarting it.

In this book, we've tried to distill down the key elements you need to get going with Couchbase. You'll get to know the internal architecture and how this affects the way you build and deploy your database system. I'll also show you how to perform key admin tasks, such as expanding your cluster and creating backups.

I've also provided a quick guide to building applications using the core protocol and document-based architecture of Couchbase Server.

Combined, all of these different sections should tell you everything you need to know to use Couchbase Server, from sizing and constructing your cluster, to deploying and expanding it. This way, when your application goes viral, you'll know what to do. Good luck!

Where to Get Help on Couchbase Server

The information provided in this book is designed as a basic guide to using Couchbase Server 1.8.

For more detailed information on Couchbase Server, you can read the full manual at *http://www.couchbase.com/docs/couchbase-manual-1.8/*. For more general information about Couchbase Server, read the website *http://www.couchbase.com*.

Information on the client libraries used to build applications against Couchbase Server, see *http://www.couchbase.com/develop*.

For a list of all the available documentation for Couchbase Server, including the upcoming Couchbase Server 2.0, see *http://www.couchbase.com/docs/*.

To get involved with the Couchbase community, there are Forums available at *http://www.couchbase.com/forums*, and a mailing list at *http://groups.google.com/group/couchbase*.

To get in touch with the author, please contact me at *editors@couchbase.com*.

Conventions Used in This Book

The following typographical conventions are used in this book:

Italic
> Indicates new terms, URLs, email addresses, filenames, and file extensions.

`Constant width`
> Used for program listings, as well as within paragraphs to refer to program elements such as variable or function names, databases, data types, environment variables, statements, and keywords.

`Constant width bold`
> Shows commands or other text that should be typed literally by the user.

`Constant width italic`
> Shows text that should be replaced with user-supplied values or by values determined by context.

 This icon signifies a tip, suggestion, or general note.

 This icon indicates a warning or caution.

Using Code Examples

This book is here to help you get your job done. In general, you may use the code in this book in your programs and documentation. You do not need to contact us for permission unless you're reproducing a significant portion of the code. For example, writing a program that uses several chunks of code from this book does not require permission. Selling or distributing a CD-ROM of examples from O'Reilly books does require permission. Answering a question by citing this book and quoting example code does not require permission. Incorporating a significant amount of example code from this book into your product's documentation does require permission.

We appreciate, but do not require, attribution. An attribution usually includes the title, author, publisher, and ISBN. For example: "*Getting Started with Couchbase Server* by MC Brown (O'Reilly). Copyright 2012 Couchbase, Inc., 978-1-449-33106-1."

If you feel your use of code examples falls outside fair use or the permission given above, feel free to contact us at *permissions@oreilly.com*.

Safari® Books Online

 Safari Books Online (*www.safaribooksonline.com*) is an on-demand digital library that delivers expert content in both book and video form from the world's leading authors in technology and business.

Technology professionals, software developers, web designers, and business and creative professionals use Safari Books Online as their primary resource for research, problem solving, learning, and certification training.

Safari Books Online offers a range of product mixes and pricing programs for organizations, government agencies, and individuals. Subscribers have access to thousands of books, training videos, and prepublication manuscripts in one fully searchable database from publishers like O'Reilly Media, Prentice Hall Professional, Addison-Wesley Professional, Microsoft Press, Sams, Que, Peachpit Press, Focal Press, Cisco Press, John Wiley & Sons, Syngress, Morgan Kaufmann, IBM Redbooks, Packt, Adobe Press, FT Press, Apress, Manning, New Riders, McGraw-Hill, Jones & Bartlett, Course Technology, and dozens more. For more information about Safari Books Online, please visit us online.

How to Contact Us

Please address comments and questions concerning this book to the publisher:

O'Reilly Media, Inc.
1005 Gravenstein Highway North
Sebastopol, CA 95472
800-998-9938 (in the United States or Canada)

707-829-0515 (international or local)
707-829-0104 (fax)

We have a web page for this book, where we list errata, examples, and any additional information. You can access this page at:

http://oreil.ly/gs-couchbase-server

To comment or ask technical questions about this book, send email to:

bookquestions@oreilly.com

For more information about our books, courses, conferences, and news, see our website at *http://www.oreilly.com*.

Find us on Facebook: *http://facebook.com/oreilly*

Follow us on Twitter: *http://twitter.com/oreillymedia*

Watch us on YouTube: *http://www.youtube.com/oreillymedia*

Acknowledgments

Writing this book would have been impossible without the stunning work by the entire Couchbase development team. They continue to put effort into new features and functionality, not to mention having designed and built the original product.

Perry Krug has given me so much input and support while producing this book, by making sure the content is correct and up to date. Without him, this book would be far less useful, not to mention inaccurate. Thanks as well to the rest of the product management team who helped to review and comment on the content.

At O'Reilly, thanks to Meghan Blanchette, my incredibly understanding and supportive editor, and Mike Loukides, who supported the inception of the book and its content.

CHAPTER 1

Introduction to Couchbase Server

Couchbase Server is a distributed, document-based database that is part of the NoSQL database movement. Couchbase Server is a persistent database that leverages an integrated RAM caching layer, enabling it to support very fast create, store, update, and retrieval operations. Couchbase is built on three core principles: Simple, Fast, Elastic.

Simple

> The core of Couchbase Server is very simple and straightforward, and from a client perspective, very easy to use. Couchbase Server is also very quick and easy to install and set up. In fact, you can generally set up a new Couchbase Server node within five minutes. Couchbase Server is also compatible with memcached; if your application already uses memcached, then you can store data in Couchbase.

> Finally, Couchbase Server builds on the basic key/value or document storage structure of memcached. This makes it very simple to store and retrieve data. You do not have to define a data structure before you start storing, and there are no complicated queries or query languages required to retrieve the data back.

Fast

> Couchbase Server is very fast. Because Couchbase Server tries to retain as much of your actively used data in memory at all times, the speed of accessing the data stored within the database is generally limited only by the network speed required to access the storage value.

> The result is that Couchbase Server supports sub-millisecond response times and has been optimized for very high-concurrency data storage. The system is linearly scalable due to a "shared nothing" architecture. You can improve the overall performance of your cluster by adding more nodes.

Elastic

> The Couchbase Server cluster is designed to be easily expanded. To create a multiple node cluster, install the software on another machine and add it to the existing cluster. You don't need to take either the cluster (or the clients and applications that are using it) down to perform this operation. The entire cluster stays running

during the process. Extending the cluster also results in linear improvements in capacity, as well as disk and network throughput.

These features are designed to support web application development where the high-performance characteristics are required to support low-latency and high throughput applications. Couchbase Server achieves this on a single server and provides support for the load to be increased almost linearly by making use of the clustered functionality built into Couchbase Server.

The cluster component distributes data over multiple servers to share the data and I/O load, while incorporating intelligence into the server and client access libraries that enable clients to quickly access the right node within the cluster for the information required. This intelligent distribution allows Couchbase Server to provide excellent scalability that can be extended simply by adding more servers as your load and application requirements increase.

Let's take a closer look at the key components that make up Couchbase Server and how they work together to provide an efficient database environment.

Architecture and Concepts

In order to understand the structure and layout of Couchbase Server, you first need to understand the different components and systems that make up both an individual Couchbase Server instance, and the components and systems that work together to make up the Couchbase Cluster as a whole.

The following section provides key information and concepts that you need to understand the fast and elastic nature of the Couchbase Server database, and how some of the components work together to support a highly available and high-performance database.

Nodes and Clusters

Couchbase Server can be used either in a standalone configuration, or in a cluster configuration where multiple Couchbase Servers are connected together to provide a single, distributed, data store.

Collectively, you can identify the components of a Couchbase system as:

Couchbase Server or node
> A single instance of the Couchbase Server software running on a machine, whether a physical machine, virtual machine, EC2 instance, or other environment.
>
> All instances of Couchbase Server are identical, provide the same functionality, interfaces and systems, and consist of the same components.

All nodes within Couchbase Server are created equally. There is no hierarchy or topology, and no single node is a 'master' of the rest of the cluster. Each node is responsible only for the data it stores and the requests made to it by clients.

Cluster

A cluster is a collection of one or more instances of Couchbase Server that are configured as a logical cluster. All nodes within the cluster are identical and provide the same functionality and information. The entire cluster shares data across the individual nodes, with each node being responsible for only a portion of the entire data set.

Clusters operate in a completely horizontal fashion. To increase the size of a cluster, you add another node. There are no parent/child relationships or hierarchical structures involved. This means that Couchbase Server scales linearly, both in terms of increasing the storage capacity and the performance and scalability.

Cluster Manager

Every node within a Couchbase Server Cluster includes the Cluster Manager component. The Cluster Manager is responsible for the following within a cluster:

- Cluster management
- Node administration
- Node monitoring
- REST API for management
- Statistics gathering and aggregation
- Runtime logging
- Multitenancy
- Security for administrative and client access

Buckets

Couchbase Server provides data management services using named buckets. These are isolated virtual containers for data. A bucket is a logical grouping of physical resources within a cluster of Couchbase Servers. They can be used by multiple client applications across a cluster. Buckets provide a secure mechanism for organizing, managing, and analyzing data storage resources.

Couchbase Server provides the two core types of buckets that can be created and managed, summarized in Table 1-1. Couchbase Server collects and reports on runtime statistics by bucket type.

Table 1-1. Bucket types

Bucket type	Description
Couchbase	Provides highly available and dynamically reconfigurable distributed data storage, providing persistence to disk and replication services. Couchbase buckets are 100% protocol compatible with Memcached.
Memcached	Provides a directly addressed, distributed (scale-out), in-memory, document cache. Memcached buckets are designed to be used alongside relational database technology—caching frequently used data, thereby reducing the number of queries a database server must perform for web servers delivering a web application.

The different bucket types support different core capabilities (as shown in Table 1-2). Couchbase-type buckets provide a highly available and dynamically reconfigurable distributed data store. Couchbase-type buckets survive node failures and allow cluster reconfiguration while continuing to service requests.

Table 1-2. Couchbase bucket capabilities

Capability	Description
Persistence	Data objects are persisted asynchronously to hard disks from memory to provide protection from server restarts or minor failures. Persistence properties are set at the bucket level.
Replication	A configurable number of replicas can receive copies of all data objects in the Couchbase-type bucket. Every node within a cluster is responsible for both active and replica data. If a node fails, the replica can be promoted to be the active container, providing continuous (HA) cluster operations via failover. Replication operates at the bucket level with replicas distributed over multiple servers in the same way as the bucket data.
Rebalancing	Rebalancing enables load distribution across resources and dynamic addition or removal of buckets and servers in the cluster.
Bucket sizing	Couchbase buckets can be sized dynamically, allowing you to change and alter the bucket size as your application needs change.

Buckets can be used to isolate individual applications to provide multitenancy, or to isolate data types to enhance performance and visibility. Couchbase Server allows you to configure different ports to access different buckets. Password authentication is also available on individual buckets.

 Smart clients discover changes in the cluster structure automatically by using the Couchbase Management REST API. This ensures that the client application continues to communicate to the appropriate node for the data being accessed.

Couchbase Server allows you to use and mix different types of buckets (Couchbase and Memcached) as appropriate in your environment. Quotas for RAM and disk usage are configurable per bucket so that resource usage can be managed across the cluster. Quotas can be modified on a running cluster so that administrators can reallocate resources as usage patterns or priorities change over time.

vBuckets

A vBucket is defined as the *owner* of a subset of the key space of a Couchbase cluster. These vBuckets are used to allow information to be distributed effectively across the cluster. The vBucket system is used both for distributing data, and for supporting replicas (copies of bucket data) on more than one node.

Clients access the information stored in a bucket by communicating directly with the node response for the corresponding vBucket. This direct access enables clients to communicate with the node storing the data, rather than using a proxy or redistribution architecture. The result is abstracting the physical topology from the logical partitioning of data. This architecture is what gives Couchbase Server elasticity.

This architecture differs from the method used by memcached, which uses client-side key hashes to determine the server from a defined list. This requires active management of the list of servers, and specific hashing algorithms such as Ketama to cope with changes to the topology. The structure is also more flexible and able to cope with changes than the typical sharding arrangement used in an RDBMS environment.

 vBuckets are not a user-accessible component, but they are a critical component of Couchbase Server and are vital to the availability support and the elastic nature.

Every document ID belongs to a vBucket. A mapping function is used to calculate the vBucket in which a given document belongs. In Couchbase Server, that mapping function is a hashing function that takes a document ID as input and outputs a vBucket identifier. Once the vBucket identifier has been computed, a table is consulted to look up the server that "hosts" that vBucket. The table contains one row per vBucket, pairing the vBucket to its hosting server. A server appearing in this table can be (and usually is) responsible for multiple vBuckets.

Data in RAM

The architecture of Couchbase Server includes a built-in caching layer. This approach allows for very fast response times, since the data is initially written to RAM by the client, and can be returned from RAM to the client when the data is requested.

The effect of this design to provide an extensive built-in caching layer that acts as a central part of the operation of the system. The client interface works through the RAM-based data store, with information stored by the clients written into RAM and data retrieved by the clients returned from RAM; or loaded from disk into RAM before being returned to the client.

This process of storing and retrieving stored data through the RAM interface ensures the best performance. For the highest performance, you should allocate the maximum amount of RAM on each of your nodes. The aggregated RAM is used across the cluster.

This is different in design from other database systems where the information is written to the database and either a separate caching layer is employed, or the caching provided by the operating system is used to keep regularly used information in memory and accessible.

Ejection

Ejection is a mechanism used with Couchbase buckets, and is the process of removing data from RAM to make room for active and more frequently used information—a key part of the caching mechanism. Ejection is automatic and operates in conjunction with the disk persistence system to ensure that data in RAM has been persisted to disk and can be safely ejected from the system.

The system ensures that the data stored in RAM will already have been written to disk, so that it can be loaded back into RAM if the data is requested by a client. Ejection is a key part of keeping frequently used information in RAM and ensuring that there is space within the Couchbase RAM allocation to load that data back into RAM when the information is requested by a client.

 For Couchbase buckets, data is never deleted from the system unless a client explicitly deletes the document from the database or the expiration value for the document is reached. Instead, the ejection mechanism removes it from RAM, keeping a copy of that information on disk.

Expiration

Each document stored in the database has an optional expiration value. The default is for there to be no expiration (i.e., the information will be stored indefinitely). The expiration can be used for data with a naturally limited life that you want to be automatically deleted from the entire database.

The expiration value is user-specified on a document basis at the point when the data is stored. The expiration can also be updated when the data is updated, or explicitly changed through the Couchbase protocol. The expiration time can either be specified as a relative time (for example, in 60 seconds), or absolute time (31st December 2012, 12:00 p.m.).

Typical uses for an expiration value include web session data, where you want the actively stored information to be removed from the system if the user activity has stopped and not been explicitly deleted. The data will time out and be removed from the system, freeing up RAM and disk for more active data.

Eviction

Eviction is the process of removing information entirely from memory for Memcached buckets. The Memcached system uses a least recently used (LRU) algorithm to remove data from the system entirely when it is no longer used.

 Within a Memcached bucket, LRU data is removed to make way for new data, with the information being deleted, since there is no persistence for Memcached buckets.

Disk Storage

For performance, Couchbase Server prefers to store and provide information to clients using RAM. However, this is not always possible or desirable in an application. Instead, what is required is the "working set" of information stored in RAM and immediately available for supporting low-latency responses.

Couchbase Server stores data on disk, in addition to keeping as much data as possible in RAM (as part of the caching layer used to improve performance). Disk persistence allows for easier backup/restore operations, and allows datasets to grow larger than the built-in caching layer.

Couchbase automatically moves data between RAM and disk (asynchronously in the background) in order to keep regularly used information in memory, and less frequently used data on disk. Couchbase constantly monitors the information accessed by clients, keeping the active data within the caching layer.

The process of removing data from the caching to make way for the actively used information is called *ejection*, and is controlled automatically through thresholds set on each configured bucket in your Couchbase Server Cluster.

The use of disk storage presents an issue in that a client request for an individual document ID must know whether the information exists or not. Couchbase Server achieves this using metadata structures. The *metadata* holds information about each document stored in the database, and this information is held in RAM. This means that the server can always return a "document ID not found" response for an invalid document ID, while returning the data for an item either in RAM (in which case it is returned immediately), or after the item has been read from disk (after a delay, or until a timeout has been reached).

The process of moving information to disk is asynchronous. Data is ejected to disk from memory in the background while the server continues to service active requests. During sequences of high writes to the database, clients will be notified that the server is temporarily out of memory until enough items have been ejected from memory to disk.

Similarly, when the server identifies an item that needs to be loaded from disk because it is not in active memory, the process is handled by a background process that processes the load queue and reads the information back from disk and into memory. The client is made to wait until the data has been loaded back into memory before the information is returned.

The asynchronous nature and use of queues in this way enables reads and writes to be handled at a very fast rate, while removing the typical load and performance spikes that would otherwise cause a traditional RDBMS to produce erratic performance.

Warmup

When Couchbase Server is restarted or when it is started after a restore from backup, the server goes through a warm-up process. The warm-up loads data from disk into RAM, making the data available to clients.

The warmup process must complete before clients can be serviced. Depending on the size and configuration of your system, and the amount of data that you have stored, the warmup may take some time to load all of the stored data into memory.

Rebalancing

The way data is stored within Couchbase Server is through the distribution offered by the vBucket structure. If you want to expand or shrink your Couchbase Server cluster, then the information stored in the vBuckets needs to be redistributed between the available nodes, with the corresponding vBucket map updated to reflect the new structure. This process is called *rebalancing*.

Rebalancing is an deliberate process that you need to initiate manually when the structure of your cluster changes. The rebalance process changes the allocation of the vBuckets used to store the information, and then physically moves the data between the nodes to match the new structure.

The rebalancing process can take place while the cluster is running and servicing requests. Clients using the cluster read and write to the existing structure, with the data being moved in the background between nodes. Once the moving process is complete, the vBucket map is updated and communicated to the smart clients and the proxy service (Moxi).

The result is that the distribution of data across the cluster has been rebalanced (or smoothed out) so that the data is evenly distributed across the database, taking into account the data and replicas of the data required to support the system.

Replicas and Replication

In addition to distributing information across the cluster for the purposes of even data distribution and performance, Couchbase Server also includes the ability to create additional replicas of the data. These replicas work in tandem with the vBucket structure, with replicas of individual vBuckets distributed data around the cluster. Distribution of replicas is handled in the same way as the core data, with portions of the data distributed around the cluster to prevent a single point of failure.

The replication of this data around this cluster is entirely peer-to-peer based, with the information being exchanged directly between nodes in the cluster. There is no topology, hierarchy, or master/slave relationship. When the data is written to a node within the cluster, the data is stored directly in the vBucket and then distributed to one or more replica vBuckets simultaneously using the TAP system.

In the event of a failure of one of the nodes in the system, the replica vBuckets are enabled in place of the vBuckets that were failed in the bad node. The process is near-instantaneous. Because the replicas are populated at the same time as the original data, there is no need for the data to be copied over; the replica vBuckets are there waiting to be enabled with the data already within them. The replica buckets are enabled and the vBucket structure updated so that clients now communicate with the updated vBucket structure.

Replicas are configured on each bucket. You can configure different buckets to contain different numbers of replicas according to the required safety level for your data. Replicas are only enabled once the number of nodes within your cluster support the required number of replicas. For example, if you configure three replicas on a bucket, the replicas will only be enabled once you have four nodes.

 The number of replicas for a bucket cannot be changed after the bucket has been created.

Failover

Information is distributed around a cluster using a series of replicas. For Couchbase buckets you can configure the number of *replicas* (complete copies of the data stored in the bucket) that should be kept within the Couchbase Server Cluster.

In the event of a failure in a server (either due to transient failure, or for administrative purposes), you can use a technique called *failover* to indicate that a node within the Couchbase Cluster is no longer available, and that the replica vBuckets for the server are enabled.

The failover process contacts each server that was acting as a replica and updates the internal table that maps client requests for documents to an available server.

Failover can be performed manually, or you can use the built-in automatic failover that reacts after a preset time when a node within the cluster becomes unavailable.

For more information, see "Failover with Couchbase" on page 69.

TAP

The TAP protocol is an internal part of the Couchbase Server system and is used in a number of different areas to exchange data throughout the system. TAP provides a stream of data of the changes that are occurring within the system.

TAP is used during replication, to copy data between vBuckets used for replicas. It is also used during the rebalance procedure to move data between vBuckets and redistribute the information across the system.

Client Interface

There are a number of client libraries available, and clients fall into two major categories, those that are smart clients, and those that are memcached-compatible. Smart clients communicate with the cluster as a whole, and information is automatically written to the correct node within the cluster according to the built-in cluster configuration and distribution of information over the vBuckets. Smart clients also communicate with the cluster to ensure that during a failover or rebalancing event, the client updates the configuration and writes to the appropriate cluster.

When using a non-smart memcached-compatible client, you must use a client-side Moxi component. The Moxi tool acts as a proxy server between your client connection and the Couchbase Server cluster. It provides the cluster level distribution and interfacing, while allowing traditional memcached clients to write to the Couchbase Cluster. Using a client-side Moxi service also enables you to take advantage of Couchbase Server functionality without changing your existing memcached application in any way.

 There are memcached clients available for a huge range of languages and environments. See *http://memcached.org*.

Within Couchbase Server, the techniques and systems used to get information into and out of the database differ according to the level and volume of data that you want to access. The different methods can be identified according to the base operations of Create, Retrieve, Update, and Delete:

Create

Information is stored into the database using the Couchbase client interface to store a *document* against a specified *document ID*. Bulk operations for setting the documents of a larger number of operations at the same time are available, and these are more efficient than multiple smaller requests.

 For basic store/retrieve operations, Couchbase Server is compatible with the memcached client protocol. For the more advanced operations, you will need to use one of the Couchbase client libraries.

The value stored can be any binary value, including structured and structured strings, serialized objects (from the native client language), or native binary data (for example, images or audio).

Retrieve

To retrieve, you must know the document ID used to store a particular value. You can also perform bulk operations to get multiple documents with the same operation, which is more efficient than multiple single requests.

Update

Updates operations include operations to update the entire document, and also to perform simple operations, such as appending or prepending information to the existing record, or incrementing and decrementing integer values.

Delete

There is a single delete operation to remove a document entirely from the database.

Smart clients are available for the following languages and environments directly from Couchbase:

- Java (*http://www.couchbase.com/develop/java/current*)
- .NET (*http://www.couchbase.com/develop/net/current*)
- PHP (*http://www.couchbase.com/develop/php/current*)
- Ruby (*http://www.couchbase.com/develop/ruby/current*)
- C [libcouchbase] (*http://www.couchbase.com/develop/c/next*)

At the time of writing, there is also an experimental Python client available, (*http://www.couchbase.com/develop/python/current*). Mark Nunberg has also written a Perl client, `Couchbase::Client`, which is based on the libcouchbase library for C. You can get more information from *https://github.com/mnunberg/perl-Couchbase-Client*.

Proxy (Moxi)

Couchbase Server includes a component called Moxi. Moxi provides a proxying service to allow traditional memcached clients to use Couchbase Server without making changes to your application or having to modify your environment to use a smart client library.

The proxy service provides connection pooling for clients and responds to topology updates within the Couchbase Server cluster to ensure that information is distributed across the cluster correctly.

If you are using one of the Couchbase clients, then you do not need to use Moxi.

 Moxi can be used in either a server-side or client-side environment. Server-side deployments involve an additional network hop, and the load and redirection of information can create problems within a production environment.

A client-side deployment, where the Moxi service is installed on each client node, is the recommended solution for production deployments.

Administration Tools

Couchbase Server was designed to be as easy to use as possible, and does not require constant attention, except for the monitoring of health status and capacity. Administration is, however, offered in a number of different tools and systems.

Couchbase Server includes three solutions for managing and monitoring your Couchbase Server and cluster:

Web administration console
Couchbase Server includes a built-in web-administration console that provides a complete interface for configuring, managing, and monitoring your Couchbase Server installation.

Command line interface
Couchbase Server includes a suite of command-line tools that provide information and control over your Couchbase Server and cluster installation. These can be used in combination with your own scripts and management procedures to provide additional functionality, such as automated failover, backups, and other procedures.

Administration REST API
Both the Web Administration Console and the command-line interfaces make use of a built-in REST API that provides the full suite of management functionality. All of the management functionality is exposed through the REST API, and as such, it acts as the authoritative interface to the server.

Because the REST interface is so complete, you can use it from your own custom management and administration scripts to support different operations.

Statistics and Monitoring

In order to understand what your cluster is doing and how it is performing, Couchbase Server incorporates a complete set of statistical and monitoring information. The statistics are provided through all of the administration interfaces.

The level of detail provided by the statistics is considerable. There is complete transparency within the system to monitor all aspects of the performance and operation of the system, allowing you to monitor and pinpoint very specific elements of your system. The structure is also granular in nature, allowing you to look at different levels of detail into different aspects of the system.

The key statistics required to monitor the health of your system are exposed through the Web Administration Console. These statistics are provided using built-in real-time graphing, allowing you to monitor the health and performance of your system.

CHAPTER 2

Installation

Couchbase Server is designed to be very easy to install, and both the initial installation and the addition of new nodes into the cluster is a straightforward process. Once the core software has been installed, you need to perform a setup process that configures your new node.

It should take no more than five minutes to get Couchbase Server up and running and in a state where you can start storing and retreiving data. There's no need to go into complex deployment or configuration stages before installing. Couchbase is designed to be expandable by simply adding more nodes to your existing cluster.

In this chapter, we'll work through the basics of building your first cluster and installing and setting up each node.

Preparation

Couchbase Server can be installed on Windows, Linux, and Mac OS X (developer only). You cannot mix platforms within the same cluster. Your cluster must be entirely Linux- or Windows-based, ideally using servers with an identical hardware configuration.

With that in mind, at the time of writing, the following are the main operating systems supported:

- RedHat Enterprise Linux 5.4 (32-bit and 64-bit)
- Ubuntu Linux 10.04 (32-bit and 64-bit)
- Windows Server 2008 (32-bit and 64-bit)

For the hardware configuration, an absolute minimum of a dual-core CPU is required. You can test Couchbase Server on machines with 1GB RAM or more, ideally 4GB RAM. Using this configuration for development and testing (but not performance testing) is fine. For full-scale deployment, you should consider a 4-core CPU and 16GB of RAM as the minimum. For more information on sizing, see "Estimating Your Cluster Size Requirements" on page 16.

Remember that Couchbase Server is designed to store your data in RAM for the best performance, so the more RAM your nodes have, the better.

For disk storage, any block-based device is fine. That is, a physical hard disk, RAID solution, SSD, or iSCSI. Using NFS or CIFS for your data storage is not supported or recommended for performance reasons.

If you want to deploy in the cloud (for example, Amazon EC2), then using the Amazon Elastic Block Store (EBS) or equivalent is fine. Within EC2, you should use the large, extra-large, or high-memory instances.

Finally, the Couchbase Server administration interface uses HTML and JavaScript, so you will need a suitable browser, such as Mozilla Firefox 3.6, Apple Safari 5, Google Chrome 11, or Internet Explorer 8. You must have JavaScript enabled.

Estimating Your Cluster Size Requirements

Couchbase Server is designed to be easily expandable as the size of your dataset and the level of your load increases. This means that you do not need to set up a large cluster before starting to use the database, and you don't need to plan the structure of your cluster either.

You can initially set up your Couchbase Server cluster with just one node for the purposes of development and testing. As you move closer to deployment, you should start to think about the more specific requirements of your cluster and the number of nodes and performance required to support your applications.

That doesn't mean that you can completely ignore the process of sizing your cluster—some basic planning now will help you deploy a better cluster in the long term.

First, you should collect some basic information about your data and application and expected activity. Collecting the following information will help:

- Number of records
- Average record size
- Expected updates per second
- Number of replicas

You can combine the first two numbers to gauge the approximate size of your dataset. For example, 10 million records of 5KB each equates to about 50GB. For best performance you'll want to keep all that data in RAM, so it's easy to estimate that machines with 16GB each means you will need at least 4 nodes. This example doesn't take into account key or metadata sizes, so be prepared to err on the side of caution.

This will give you your basic dataset size. For each replica, will need to increase the size accordingly. For example, if you calculate a 20GB data set, and have configured 1 replica, you will need 40GB (20GB for the data, 20GB for the replica of that data). For 3 replicas, you will need 80GB.

The storage used by each document within Couchbase Server includes an overhead that contains metadata about the document that must be kept in memory at all times, even if the data itself has been ejected from memory. Although the overhead is comparatively small (approximately 140 bytes), with a very large dataset the overall effect can be significant. For example, one billion records requires 130GB of RAM for the metadata.

For the disk I/O, you will need to compare the expected update rate with the type of disk you are using. Getting into the details is beyond the scope of this book (check the Couchbase Server manual for more details), but SSDs have about four times the performance of a typical hard disk. We recommend an average hard disk rate of 1500 operations per second, so if you expect to handle 15,000 updates a second, you'll need ten machines to cope with the updates.

RAM or I/O bound clusters

Keeping this basic information in mind, within Couchbase there are two primary considerations when thinking about your cluster size:

Amount of data to be stored, and how much you want to keep in RAM
If your dataset is large but your update rate low, your cluster will likely be limited by RAM rather than disk I/O, and you can estimate the size requirements of your cluster by dividing the total size of your dataset by the RAM allocated to Couchbase on each machine.

Quantity of writes and updates
The number of writes and updates to your dataset will affect the disk I/O required to persist the information down to disk. If the number of updates to your dataset is high, then your application and Couchbase cluster will likely be I/O-limited. It's critical to the health and performance of your cluster that Couchbase is capable of keeping up with the writes.

You should choose whichever calculation results in the highest number of nodes for your requirements. That is, if your update rate indicates you need 10 machines, but your RAM requirements recommend only 4, you need 10 nodes in your cluster.

For more accurate sizing information and advice, you should read the information and equations provided in the Couchbase Server manual. See Couchbase Server Sizing Guidelines (*http://www.couchbase.com/docs/couchbase-manual-1.8/couchbase-bestpractice-sizing.html*).

Fortunately, as I've already described, Couchbase is capable of expanding and contracting with ease. The answer to both the RAM and I/O problems is the same. Because Couchbase exhibits near-linear scalability, if you find you are running out of either RAM or disk I/O, you can add additional nodes to the cluster.

Adding new nodes to the cluster does not require that your cluster be taken down; you can do the entire process while the cluster is running and servicing requests from your application clients.

You can learn more about the basic process of shrinking and expanding your cluster in Chapter 6.

Network Ports

Couchbase Server uses the ports shown in the table below for communication, both with clients and for communication between nodes within the cluster. The list of ports, and which components need them, are listed in Table 2-1.

In the table, the corresponding port will need to be available on the server for Couchbase Server to run properly. If you are using a firewall, you must make sure that these ports are open for communication.

Table 2-1. Network ports used by Couchbase Server

Port	Purpose	Couchbase Server	Couchbase Client	REST API Client
8091	Web Administration Port	Yes	Yes	Yes
11210	Data Port	Yes	Yes	No
4369	Erlang Port Mapper (epmd)	Yes	No	No
21100 to 21199 (inclusive)	Internal Cluster Port	Yes	No	No

Installing Couchbase Server

To install Couchbase Server on your machine, you must download the appropriate package for your chosen platform from *http://www.couchbase.com/downloads*. For each platform, follow the corresponding platform-specific instructions.

Red Hat Linux Installation

The RedHat installation uses the RPM package. Installation is supported on RedHat and RedHat-based operating systems such as CentOS.

To install, use the `rpm` command-line tool with the RPM package that you downloaded. You must be logged in as root (Superuser) to complete the installation:

```
root-shell> rpm --install couchbase-server-version.rpm
```

version is the version number of the downloaded package.

Once the `rpm` command has been executed, the Couchbase Server starts, and is configured to automatically start during boot under the 2, 3, 4, and 5 runlevels. Refer to the RedHat RPM documentation for more information about installing packages using RPM.

Once installation has completed, the installation process will display a message similar to the following:

```
Starting Couchbase server: [ OK ]

You have successfully installed Couchbase Server.
Please browse to http://hostname:8091/ to configure your server.
Please refer to http://couchbase.com/support for
additional resources.

Please note that you have to update your firewall configuration to
allow connections to the following ports: 11211, 11210, 4369, 8091
and from 21100 to 21199.

By using this software you agree to the End User License Agreement.
See /opt/couchbase/LICENSE.txt.
```

Once installed, you can use the RedHat `chkconfig` command to manage the Couchbase Server service, including checking the current status and creating the links to enable and disable automatic startup. Refer to the RedHat documentation for instructions.

To continue installation, you should follow the server setup instructions. See "Setting Up Couchbase Server" on page 21.

Ubuntu Linux Installation

The Ubuntu installation uses the DEB package.

To install, use the `dpkg` command-line tool using the DEB file that you downloaded. The following example uses `sudo`, which will require root-access to allow installation:

```
shell> sudo dpkg -i couchbase-server-version.deb
```

version is the version number of the downloaded package.

Once the `dpkg` command has been executed, the Couchbase Server starts, and is configured to automatically start during boot under the 2, 3, 4, and 5 runlevels. Refer to the Ubuntu documentation for more information about installing packages using the Debian package manager.

Once installation has completed, the installation process will display a message similar to the following:

```
Selecting previously unselected package couchbase-server.
(Reading database ... 150475 files and directories currently installed.)
Unpacking couchbase-server (from couchbase-server-community_x86_64_1.8.0.deb) ...
Setting up couchbase-server (1.8.0r) ...
 * Started couchbase-server
```

```
You have successfully installed Couchbase Server.
Please browse to http://mc-ubuntu:8091/ to configure your server.
Please refer to http://couchbase.com for additional resources.

Please note that you have to update your firewall configuration to
allow connections to the following ports: 11211, 11210, 4369, 8091
and from 21100 to 21299.

By using this software you agree to the End User License Agreement.
See /opt/couchbase/LICENSE.txt.
```

Once installed, you can use the `service` command to manage the Couchbase Server service, including checking the current status. Refer to the Ubuntu documentation for instructions.

To continue installation, you should follow the server setup instructions. See "Setting Up Couchbase Server" on page 21.

Microsoft Windows Installation

To install on Windows, you must download the Windows installer package (MSI). This is supplied as an Windows executable. Double-click on the downloaded executable file and go through the following steps:

1. The installer will launch and prepare for installation. You can cancel this process at any time. Once completed, you will be provided with the welcome screen.

2. Click Next to start the installation. You will be prompted with the Installation Location screen. You can change the location where the Couchbase Server application is located. Note that this does not configure the location where the persistent data will be stored, only the location of the application itself.

3. Click Next to confirm the installation and start the installation process.

4. The install will copy over the necessary files to the system. During the installation process, the installer will also check to ensure that the default administration port is not already in use by another application. If the default port is unavailable, the installer will prompt for a different port to be used for administration of the Couchbase Server.

5. Once the installation process has been completed, you will be prompted with the completion screen. When you click Finish, the installer will quit and automatically open a web browser with the Couchbase Server setup window.

 Although not covered here, you can also install the package from the command line, in addition to using the traditional UI.

To continue installation, you should follow the server setup instructions. See "Setting Up Couchbase Server" on page 21.

Setting Up Couchbase Server

Once you've installed Couchbase Server, you need to follow the basic setup process. This process can be completed either through a web browser, through the command line, or by using the REST API. The setup configures your Couchbase Server installation, including setting the memory settings, disk locations, and optionally allowing you to join an existing cluster. The process is identical on each platform.

> If you are adding a node to an existing cluster, you need only set the disk location for the storage of information.

To start the configuration and setup process using the web browser, you should open the Couchbase Web Console. On Windows, this is opened for you automatically. You can access the web console on all platforms by connecting to the embedded web server on port 8091. For example, if your server can be identified on your network as `servera`, you can access the web console by opening `http://servera:8091/`. You can also use an IP address or, if you are on the same machine, `http://localhost:8091`. Then follow these steps:

1. When you open the web console for the first time immediately after installation, you will be prompted with the screen shown in Figure 2-1. Click the SETUP button to start the setup process.

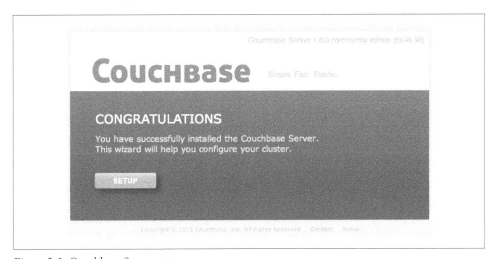

Figure 2-1. Couchbase Server setup

2. First, you must set the disk storage and cluster configuration using the screen shown in Figure 2-2. The sections are explained here:

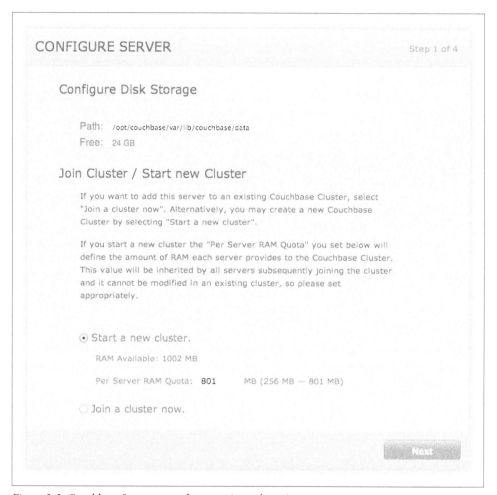

Figure 2-2. Couchbase Server setup, first step (new cluster)

Configure Disk Storage
  The *Configure Disk Storage* option specifies the location of the persistent (on-disk) storage used by Couchbase Server. The setting affects only this server and sets the directory where all the data will be stored on disk.

Join Cluster/Start New Cluster
  The *Configure Server Memory* section sets the amount of physical RAM that will be allocated by Couchbase Server for storage.

If you are creating a new cluster, you specify the memory that will be allocated on each node within your Couchbase cluster. You must specify a value that will be supported on all the nodes in your cluster, as this is a global setting.

If you want to join an existing cluster, a different configuration is shown (see Figure 2-3); select the radio button. This will change the display and prompt you to enter the IP address of an existing node, as well as the username and password of an administrator with rights to access the cluster. The setup process will complete if you use this method.

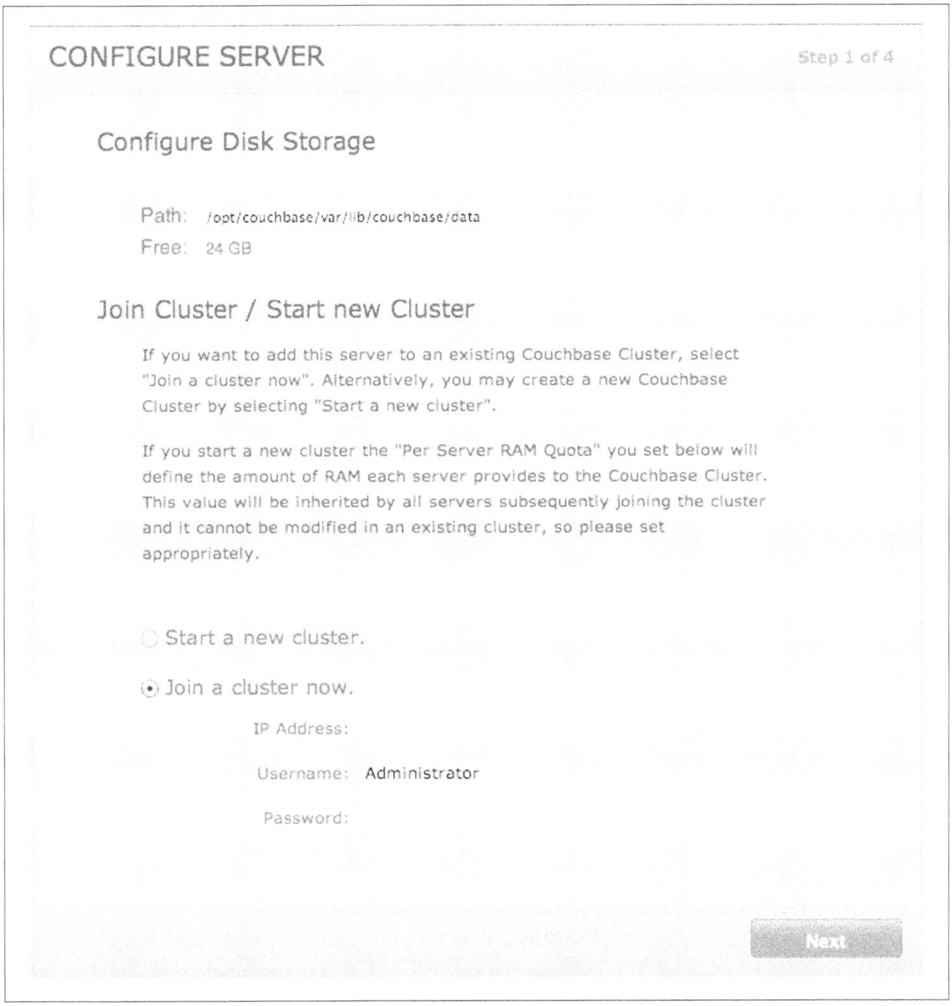

CONFIGURE SERVER   Step 1 of 4

Configure Disk Storage

Path: /opt/couchbase/var/lib/couchbase/data
Free: 24 GB

Join Cluster / Start new Cluster

If you want to add this server to an existing Couchbase Cluster, select "Join a cluster now". Alternatively, you may create a new Couchbase Cluster by selecting "Start a new cluster".

If you start a new cluster the "Per Server RAM Quota" you set below will define the amount of RAM each server provides to the Couchbase Cluster. This value will be inherited by all servers subsequently joining the cluster and it cannot be modified in an existing cluster, so please set appropriately.

○ Start a new cluster.

⦿ Join a cluster now.

IP Address:

Username: Administrator

Password:

Next

Figure 2-3. Couchbase Server setup, first step (existing cluster)

Click Next to continue the installation process.

3. Next, you need to configure a default bucket for the server (see Figure 2-4). You can delete this bucket after installation if you don't need or want it.

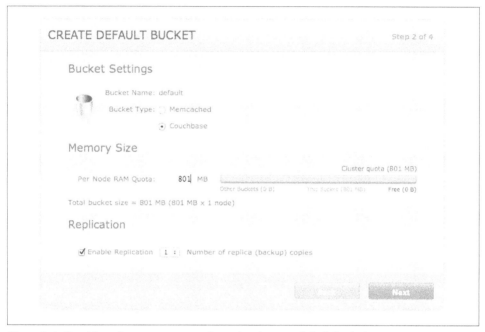

Figure 2-4. Couchbase Server setup, second step (configuring default bucket)

The options are:

Bucket Type

Specifies the type of the bucket to be created. You should choose Couchbase to take advantage of the scalability characteristics of Couchbase Server.

The remainder of the options differ based on your selection.

When selecting the Couchbase bucket type:

Memory Size

This option specifies the amount of available RAM configured on this server, which should be allocated to the default bucket.

Replication

For Couchbase buckets, you can enable replicas for a bucket. You can configure up to three replicas. When enabled, replicas of the information stored in a bucket are kept on additional nodes in the cluster, allowing for these replicas to be used in event of a node failure. The replica can be promoted to take its place, providing continuous (high-availability) cluster operations in spite of machine failure.

You can disable replicas by setting the number of replica copies to zero (0).

Click Next to continue the setup process.

4. In Step 3, you can optionally enable the notification system within the Couchbase Web Console (see Figure 2-5).

Figure 2-5. Couchbase Server setup, third step (enabling notification system)

If you select the *Update Notifications* option, the Web Console checks the version number of your installation with the latest released version. During this process, the client submits the following information to the Couchbase Server:

The current version of your Couchbase Server installation
When a new version of Couchbase Server becomes available, you will be provided with a notification of the new version and information on where you can download it.

Basic information about the size and configuration of your Couchbase cluster
This information will be used to help prioritize development efforts.

The process occurs within the browser accessing the web console, not within the server itself, and no further configuration or Internet access is required on the server to enable this functionality. If the client accessing the Couchbase Server console has Internet access, the information can be communicated correctly.

The update notification process the information anonymously, and the data cannot be tracked. The information is only used to provide you with update notifications and collect data that will help improve the future development process for Couchbase Server and related products.

Enterprise Edition

You can also register your product from within the setup process. On Enterprise Editions of Couchbase Server, you can optionally select that Couchbase, Inc. plants a tree as a thank you for completing the registration process. For more information on the tree planting sponsorship program, see Mokugift (*http://www.mokugift.com/*), supported by the United Nations Environment Program.

To have your tree planted, fill in your email address, name, and company details, and tick the "Yes, please plant my tree!" checkbox.

Community Edition

Supplying your email address will add you to the Couchbase community mailing list, which will provide you with news and update information about Couchbase and related products. You can unsubscribe from the mailing list at any time using the unsubscribe link provided in each email communication.

Click Next to continue the setup process.

5. The final step in the setup process is shown in Figure 2-6. You must configure the username and password for the administrator of the server. The same credentials are also used for the Couchbase Management REST API. Enter a username and password. The password must be at least six characters in length.

Click Next to continue the complete the process.

Once the setup process has been completed, you will be presented with the Couchbase Web Console showing the Cluster Overview page, shown in Figure 2-7.

Your Couchbase Server is now running and ready to use.

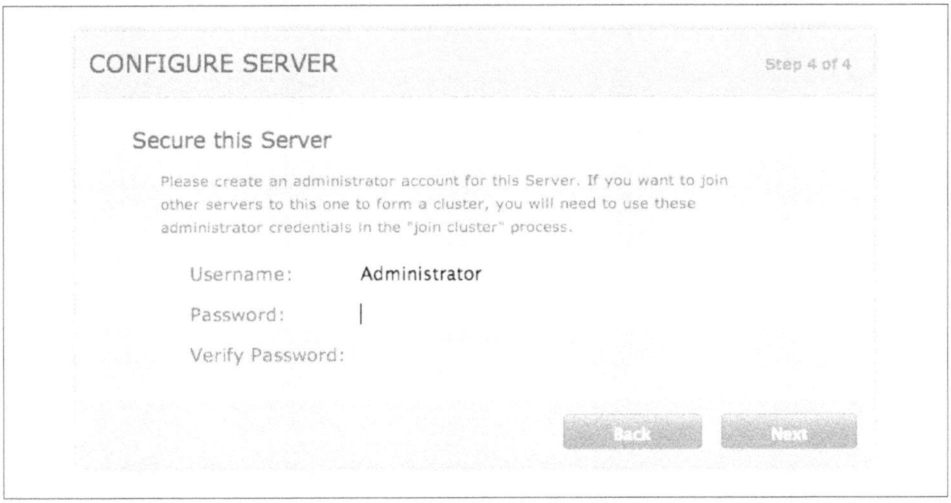

Figure 2-6. Couchbase Server setup, fourth step (configuring username and password)

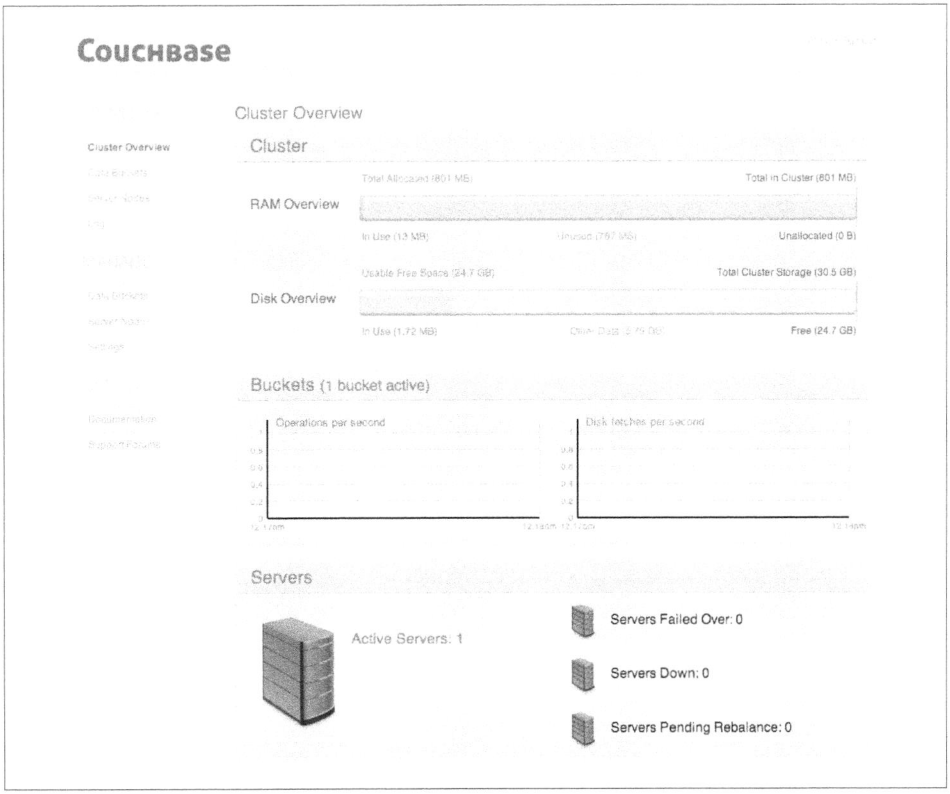

Figure 2-7. Couchbase Server setup completed

CHAPTER 3

Couchbase Administration Console

The Couchbase Administration Console will normally be your first interaction with Couchbase Server and you should familiarize yourself with the console and the combination of information and mangement tools it provides.

Couchbase Server incorporates three different administration tools: a REST-based API, a suite of command-line tools, and the web-based Administration Console. Both the Web Console and the command-line interfaces use the common REST API for their functionality.

The administration console is the easiest of the interfaces to use and provides a complete environment for management and monitoring of Couchbase, including live statistics and graphs showing the status and health of your cluster.

 The REST API and associated command-line tools enable you to automate the administration and monitoring of your console. Because the entire administration interface is based on the REST API, the entire administration system is scriptable or controllable through the command line or your chosen application environment. Check the Couchbase Manual for details of these two components.

The Administration Console is divided into two major sections, one for monitoring your cluster and one for managing your cluster. The major sections divide the information according to whether you want to monitor or manage the cluster. The common elements in both major sections are those related to the data buckets and server nodes.

- The *Cluster Overview* provides a quick guide to the status of your Couchbase cluster and is the home page when you first log on to your cluster.
- *Data Buckets* provides access to your data bucket configuration, including creating new buckets, editing existing configurations, and giving detailed analysis and statistics on the bucket activity.

- *Server Nodes* details your active nodes and their configuration and activity. You can also add new nodes, fail over nodes, remove nodes from your cluster, and view server-specific performance and monitoring statistics.

In the following sections we'll look at some of the key areas of the user interface. We'll also take the opportunity to examine the statistics provided by Couchbase Server, as well as some of the key values and events to look out for when running your cluster.

Cluster Overview

The Cluster Overview page shown in Figure 3-1 is the home page for the Couchbase Web Console. The page is designed to give you a quick overview of your cluster health, including your servers, RAM and disk usage, and cluster activity.

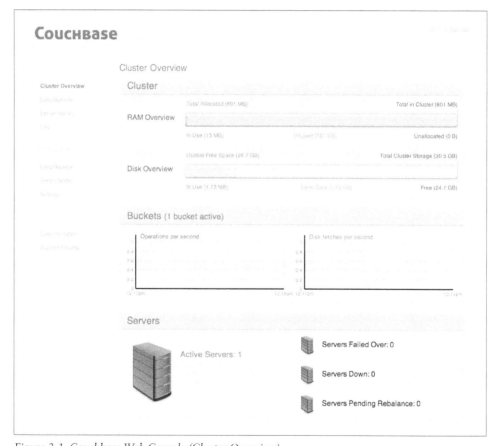

Figure 3-1. Couchbase Web Console (Cluster Overview)

Cluster

The Cluster section provides RAM and disk usage information for your cluster. The RAM portion of this section provides basic information on the RAM status of your entire cluster. You should use this to determine whether you are getting the best performance and whether your cluster is nearing RAM capacity, which means you should consider expanding your cluster.

Total in Cluster
>   Total RAM configured within the cluster. This is the total amount of memory configured for all the servers within the cluster.

Total Allocated
>   The amount of RAM allocated to data buckets within your cluster.

Unallocated
>   The amount of RAM not allocated to data buckets within your cluster.

In Use
>   The amount of memory across all buckets that is actually in use (i.e., data is actively being stored).

Unused
>   The amount of memory that is unused (available) for storing data.

The *Disk Overview* section provides similar summary information for disk storage space across your cluster.

Total Cluster Storage
>   Total amount of disk storage available across your entire cluster for storing data.

Usable Free Space
>   The amount of usable space for storing information on disk. This figure shows the amount of space available on the configured path after non-Couchbase files have been taken into account.

Other Data
>   The quantity of disk space in use by data other than Couchbase information.

In Use
>   The amount of disk space Couchbase is using to actively store information on disk.

Free
>   The free space available for storing objects on disk.

Buckets

The Buckets section provides two graphs showing the *Operations per second* and *Disk fetches per second*.

The *Operations per second* provides information on the level of activity on the cluster in terms of storing or retrieving objects from the data store.

The *Disk fetches per second* indicates how frequently Couchbase has to go to disk to retrieve information instead of using the information stored in RAM.

Servers

The Servers section indicates overall server information for the cluster:

- *Active Servers* is the number of active servers within the current cluster configuration.
- *Servers Failed Over* is the number of servers that have failed over due to an issue that should be investigated.
- *Servers Down* shows the number of servers that are down and not contactable.
- *Servers Pending Rebalance* shows the number of servers that are currently waiting to be rebalanced after joining a cluster or being reactivated after failover.

Manage: Data Buckets

To manage the configuration of your Data Buckets, use the Manage section of the web console. This shows the Ram Usage, Quota, and overall Disk Usage for each data bucket. You can obtain detailed information about the status of your data buckets by clicking on the bucket name button within the Data Buckets page. The bucket information shows memory size, access, and replica information for the bucket, as shown in Figure 3-2.

You can edit the bucket information by clicking the Edit button within the bucket information display.

To create a new data bucket, click the Create New Data Bucket button. To edit an existing bucket, click the Edit button within the detailed bucket display. See the next section for details on creating new data buckets.

Creating and Editing Data Buckets

When creating a new data bucket, or editing an existing one, you will be presented with the bucket configuration screen. From here, you can set the memory size, access control (and other settings, depending on whether you are editing or creating a new bucket), and the bucket type.

Creating a new bucket

When creating a new bucket, you are presented with the Create Bucket dialog, as shown in Figure 3-3.

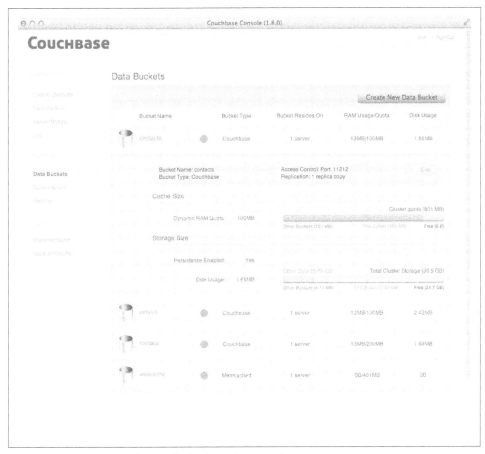

Figure 3-2. Couchbase Web Console (bucket information)

Bucket Name

The bucket name. The bucket name can only contain characters in range A-Z, a-z, 0-9 as well as underscore, period, dash, and percent symbols.

Bucket Type

Specifies the type of the bucket to be created, either Memcached or Couchbase.

Access Control

The access control configures the port your clients will use to communicate with the data bucket, and whether the bucket requires a password.

To use a server-side proxy port, select the dedicated port radio button and enter the port number you want to use. Using a dedicated port supports both the text and binary client protocols, and does not require authentication.

Create Bucket   ✕

Bucket Settings

        Bucket Name: |_____| Bucket name cannot be empty

        Bucket Type: ⦾ Memcached
                     ⦿ Couchbase

Access Control

  ⦿ Standard port (TCP port 11211. Needs SASL auth.)

     Enter password:

  ⦾ Dedicated port (supports ASCII protocol and is auth-less)

     Protocol Port:

Memory Size

                                               Cluster quota (801 MB)

  Per Node RAM Quota: 201 MB ▓▓▓▓▓▓▓▓▓▓▓▓▓▓▓▓▓▓▓▓▓▓▓▓▓▓▓▓▓▓
                           Other Buckets (600 MB)   This Bucket (201 MB)   Free (0 B)

Total bucket size = 201 MB (201 MB × 1 node)

Replication

   ☑ Enable Replication   [1 ▾] Number of replica (backup) copies
                  Warning, you do not have enough servers to support the number of replicas.

                                         Cancel   **Create**

Figure 3-3. Couchbase Web Console (Create Bucket dialog)

 Server-side proxying is not recommended for deployment. You should either use a "smart" client that uses the Couchbase protocol, or use a client-side proxy.

Memory Size
    This option specifies the amount of available RAM configured on each server that should be allocated to the bucket being configured.

Replication
    For Couchbase buckets, you can enable replica support by setting the number of replicas required for this bucket. You can disable replication by setting the number of replica copies to zero (0).

Once you have selected the options for the new bucket, you can click the Create button to create and activate the bucket within your cluster. You can cancel the bucket creation using the Cancel button.

Editing Couchbase buckets

You can edit a limited number of settings for an existing Couchbase bucket:

- *Access Control*, including the standard port/password or custom port settings.
- *Memory Size* can be modified, provided that you have unallocated space within your Cluster configuration. You can reduce the amount of memory allocated to a bucket if that space is not already in use.

The bucket name cannot be modified. If you need to change the bucket name, the only way to do this is to delete the existing bucket and create a new bucket with the new name. This will remove the data stored in the bucket. You should take a backup of the bucket data if you want to keep the information.

To delete the configured bucket entirely, click the Delete button.

Editing Memcached buckets

For Memcached buckets, you can modify the following settings when editing an existing bucket:

- *Access Control*, including the standard port/password or custom port settings.

You can delete the bucket entirely by clicking the Delete button.

You can empty a Memcached bucket of all the cached information that it stores by using the Flush button.

 Using the Flush button removes all the objects stored in the Memcached bucket. Using this button on active Memcached buckets may delete important information.

Couchbase Server States

Couchbase Server nodes can be in a number of different states depending on their current activity and availability. The displayed states are:

Up
   Host is up, replicating data between nodes and servicing requests from clients.

Down
   If a host is down, it won't replicate data between nodes or service requests from clients, as you can see in Figure 3-4.

Figure 3-4. Down status

Pending

The pending state indicates that although the server is recognized as communicable, it is not currently servicing requests. Normally, this is because the node has been added or removed from the cluster and requires a rebalance operation. It may also indicate a node in a state of warming up or a transient error.

You can monitor the current server status using both the *Manage: Server Nodes* and *Monitor: Server Nodes* screens within the Web Console.

CHAPTER 4

Developing with Couchbase

When building an application with Couchbase, your first consideration should be how you communicate and integrate with the Couchbase cluster. From a client perspective, your Couchbase cluster should operate like a "black box" environment. Although you need to be aware of the environment in which you are operating, the configuration, topology, and scope of your cluster is irrelevant to the way you will store and retrieve information.

You configure your client to communicate with the cluster and store data. The client library (or the Moxi proxy service) is responsible for the communication to individual nodes within the cluster to handle the distribution of data. Other aspects, such as rebalancing or failover, should not affect or interrupt the core operations of exchanging information.

In this chapter we're going to start by taking a quick look at how the basic storage operations work, then look more closely at the key operations supported within Couchbase Server on the stored data, and then discuss some of the main considerations when developing an application that uses the document model with Couchbase Server to store data.

Hello Couchbase

Couchbase Server stores information by storing a document (the value) identified by a document ID (the key). This makes the development and deployment of your application very simple. You store a document by sending the document data and the document ID you want to store it under. To get the information back, you provide the document ID and get the exact data you stored back again.

Providing you know the ID of the document you want to retrieve, you can always get the information back. The data is stored simply as a sequence of bytes. This means that you can either store raw information (such as a string or integer), more complex structures (such as JavaScript Object Notation [JSON]), or serialized objects. Serialization converts native objects for your given language into a suitable bytestring that can then be materialized back into a object when it has been retrieved from the server.

The basic storage and retrieval process is therefore very simple. For the examples below I've used Ruby, although all the different client languages work in the same fashion since they all use the same core protocol.

 You can get downloads of all the Couchbase client libraries from *http: //www.couchbase.com/develop*. For Ruby specifically, follow the instructions on *http://couchbase.com/develop/ruby/current*.

With the Couchbase client library for Ruby installed, you can create and build a simple program to store and then retrieve information in your Couchbase Server. A sample program, *hello-world.rb*, is shown in Example 4-1.

Example 4-1. Hello World!

```ruby
require 'rubygems'
require 'couchbase'

client = Couchbase.new "http://127.0.0.1:8091/pools/default"
client.quiet = false
begin
  spoon = client.get "spoon"
  puts spoon
rescue Couchbase::Error::NotFound => e
  puts "There is no spoon."
  client.set "spoon", "Hello World!", :ttl => 10
end
```

Dissecting the script reveals the **set** and **get** process common in Couchbase:

- The first two lines load the necessary libraries.
- The next line opens up a connection to your Couchbase Cluster. The definition is through a URL which should point to at least one node within your cluster. In this example, the `localhost` address is used. The bucket name, `default`, is explicitly requested. You can change this to another bucket if you have configured it.
- The remainder of the script performs a retrieve and store operation. If the initial retrieve operation (for the document ID `"spoon"`) fails, then we set the data into the database. If the document ID does exist, the script prints out the stored value.

You can test this script out by running it from the command line. The first time you run it, it should output this error string:

```
shell> ruby hello-world.rb
There is no spoon.
```

The specified document does not exist in the database, but is added after the error string has been printed. The second time you run it, you should get the stored document value:

```
shell> ruby hello-world.rb
Hello World!
```

As an additional demonstration, the welcome string stored has been given an expiry value of 10 seconds. This means that if you wait longer than 10 seconds after you have stored the value, the value will be deleted from the database. If you wait more than 10 seconds from the first time you ran the script and execute the script again, it should output this error string:

```
shell> ruby hello-world.rb
There is no spoon.
```

Although this is a very basic example, it demonstrates the simplicity of retrieving and storing information into Couchbase Server using the basic get/set operations.

Deployment Options

To get the best out of Couchbase Server and the client environment that you are using, you should use one of the Couchbase clients. These "smart" clients combine the core interface protocol used for storing information with the administration protocol. The latter enables the clients to communicate directly with the Couchbase cluster to understand the vBucket map so that information can be sent directly to individual nodes within the cluster. The same system also allows for changes to the vBucket map to be acted upon during failover and rebalance scenarios.

There are six client libraries supported directly by Couchbase:

- Java
- .NET
- PHP
- Ruby
- C (libcouchbase)
- Python

Each of these clients is a "smart" client, providing you with the best combination of key functionality and intelligent support of the cluster configuration and operation. You can get more information at *http://www.couchbase.com/develop*.

If you want to use a memcached-compatible library or application that you have already written that uses this protocol, but which takes advantage of the Couchbase Server cluster architecture, then you can use the Moxi service.

The Moxi proxy service interfaces between the memcached protocol and a Couchbase Server cluster. Couchbase Server is 100% memcached-compatible at a protocol level. To do this, you should install Moxi on each client, configure the Moxi service to connect to your Couchbase Server cluster, and then connect to Moxi using localhost as the hostname. For more information, see the Couchbase Server manual (*http://www.couch base.com/docs*).

 Although Couchbase Server is memcached protocol-compliant, there are additional operations within the Couchbase protocol that are not supported by memcached, which you will obviously not be able to take advantage of.

Basic Operations

Couchbase Server operates as a document store with a very simple store/retrieve model based on the ID that you give for each document. There are no tables or structures to define when you store the information, and there are no complicated queries to write to get information in and out.

All operations within Couchbase Server follow some basic rules:

All operations are atomic
> This means that there are no locking mechanisms within the server, and there is no possibility of simultaneous commands from multiple clients corrupting the stored data. However, this also means that if multiple clients perform a set operation, it is the last one that will remain active when the operations have completed.
>
> To manage concurrency and race conditions, you can use the CAS operations. These require an additional checksum value so that the values cannot be updated without supplying a suitable valid checksum.

All data operation require a key
> All operations require the key name of the data being updated or retrieved. You cannot perform a global operation or an operation on multiple keys (with the exception of the multiple-get).

No implicit locking
> There is no implicit locking within the system when storing or updating data. The operation will either complete successfully, or fail for a reason unrelated to the individual key/value pair (for example, a temporary out of memory error).

The different client languages and implementations work with the core protocol to communicate with Couchbase Server:

All clients implement the core protocol
> Although there are some differences in the exact structure and function names used by different languages and environments, they all implement the same core protocol operations. For example, the set() protocol call is available in all implementations, although some clients may use the term "store."

Function call structure differences

Due to the differences in the different languages and environments, the exact function structure may be different from the core protocol. For example, within Java, where variable-argument methods are not available, there are multiple variants of the same function. In other languages, such as Perl, Python, and Ruby, where hashes are core variable types, these are often used for storing and returning information.

Different languages implement additional functionality

Related to the two previous examples, some of the client implementations provide additional function calls and structures that are not supported by the core protocol. For example, within Java, all operations are available as both synchronous and asynchronous operations, enabling you to continue processing information while get or set operations are executing.

Not all implementations support flags

The flags, stored by the server along with the value and specified key, are not supported by all the different client libraries.

The core protocol and operations supported with Couchbase are shown in Table 4-1.

Table 4-1. Core protocol operations

Operation	Description
add(key, value [,expiry])	Adds a new value if the key does not exist, or returns an error.
set(key, value [,expiry])	Sets a value, whether the key already exists or not.
get(key)	Gets a value using the supplied key.
getAndTouch(key, expiry)	Gets a value, and updates the expiry time.
getBulk(key [,key, ..., keyn])	Get multiple values simultaneously. More efficient than multiple single get operations.
gets(key)	Get the value and CAS for a given key.
replace(key, value [,expiry])	Replaces an existing value if the specified key exists.
append(key, value)	Append data to an existing key/value pair.
prepend(key, value)	Prepend data to an existing key/value pair.
increment(key, value [, offset])	Increment a stored integer by a specified value (default 1)
decrement(key, value [, offset])	Decrement a stored integer by a specified value (default 1)
touch(key, expiry)	Update the expiry time for a given value
cas(key, value, checksum)	Updates a document only when the supplied checksum matches the one stored on the server
delete(key)	Deleted the specified document

Regardless of the client library, the functions work the same across the different languages, with some differences to account for conventions. For example, you can increment a value within Ruby using:

```
couchbase.incr("counter", 5)
```

Within .NET, the function call is:

```
client.Increment("counter", 100, 1);
```

The second argument in this case is the default value if the specified document ID does not already exist.

Compare and Swap (Check and Set)

In addition to the core functions, there is one special function called compare and swap (or check and set, or compare and swap, depending on who you talk to!). Compare and swap provides a checksum that ensures multiple clients do not update a document that may have subsequently changed on the server since the document was last fetched.

For example, consider the following scenario:

1. Client A gets the value for the document "Martin".
2. Client B gets the value for the document "Martin".
3. Client A adds information to the document value and updates it.
4. Client B adds information to the document value and updates it.

In the above sequence, the update by Client B will overwrite the information in the database, removing the data that Client A added.

To provide a solution to this, you can use the compare and swap (`cas()`) function. This requires that a unique CAS value be retrieved from the server. The CAS value is changed every time the document is updated, even if the document is updated to the same value. When sending the update to the server, if the CAS value known by the client does not match the CAS value currently stored for the document, then the operation will fail.

The result is a change to the above sequence:

1. Client A gets the value for the document "Martin" and the CAS value.
2. Client B gets the value for the document "Martin" and the CAS value.
3. Client A adds information to the document value and updates it, using the CAS value as a check. The document is updated.
4. Client B adds information to the document value and tries to update it using the CAS value. The operation fails, because the cached CAS value on client B is now different from the CAS value on the server after the update by client A.

CAS therefore supports an additional level of checking and verifies that the information you are updating matches the copy of the information you originally retrieved.

Within your code, CAS is a function just like the update() function. Depending on your environment, you may need to use a special get function (`gets()`) that obtains both the document information and CAS value.

For example, within Java you would update an existing document through CAS first by getting the value and stored CAS value, and then using the `cas()` method to update the document:

```
CASValue customer = client.gets("customer");
CASResponse casr = client.cas("customer", customer.getCas(), "new string value");
```

The limitation of using CAS is that it is not enforceable at an application client library level. If you want to use it for all the update operations, you must explicitly use it over the standard document update functions.

Storing Data in Couchbase Server

Couchbase Server is strictly a document database. That is, information is stored in the database according to the document ID (used to reference the data), and the corresponding document value. This means that there is no need to expressly set the format of the data, create a schema, or even tell Couchbase Server about the information that you are storing.

All you need to do is store document data against a document ID that you specify.

Because of the document structure, there are some different considerations when building and developing your applications. Let's start by taking a look at the basics of the document ID and document value.

Document IDs

The document ID (or key) used to store your data is important. Keys must be unique within a bucket (because they must uniquely identify the content of the corresponding value).

The key should be used to identify the information and can be any string, generally up to 128 characters in length. There are no mechanisms within Couchbase Server to create a unique or sequential ID. If you want to use a UUID you will need to use a library within your chosen application environment.

It also standard practice to use a prefix, type, and/or a separator to different information that you store into each bucket. For example, you might store information about a beer by using an ID like `beer_9834759`. Here the `beer` prefix identifies the record type, and the underscore acts as a separator between that and the unique beer ID.

Within the same bucket you could add `brewery_893749` to store brewery information and differentiate that from the beer records.

Couchbase Server 1.8 does not support the ability to get the list of document IDs within a bucket, or to iterate over the documents stored in the database in any way. You also cannot perform queries or lookups on the information except by knowing the ID. However, this functionality will be supported in the forthcoming Couchbase Server 2.0 release.

One way to simplify this is to enable your application to create and produce links of the information. For example, when a new beer record is added to the database, you can update a document called `beer_list` that contains a list of the individual beer records. Because updates are atomic, it should be possible to keep an up-to-date manual list of this information. The same basic principle can also be used to link records in the database. For example of this in action, see *https://blog.couchbase.com/maintaining-set -memcached*.

Your application should be able to bootstrap itself by using and reading this fixed-named record, either by reading a local configuration or by storing a configuration record into the bucket.

Document Data

The data stored within a document is purely a sequence of bytes. The server makes no attempt to parse or understand the information being stored into the document. This means that you can store everything from numbers up to images.

The open-ended structure of the information means that there is no need to declare or define the structure of the information that you want to store. It also gives you the ultimate flexibility to determine the structure of the information.

To store simple information, such as a number or a string, you can simply write the data into the document value.

To store more complicated structures of information, you will want to use either native object serialization or a generic structure such as JSON.

Serialization

Serialization converts a complicated internal structure, such as a hash or object from your client language, and converts it into a sequence of bytes that can be stored within Couchbase Server's document database structure.

More usefully, serialized structures can also be deserialized back into their internal, language-specific, format so that they can be used natively within your application.

All the Couchbase Server client libraries automatically support serialization and deserialization of a structure or object supplied to them within the storage and retrieve methods.

JSON

The problem with serialization of information is that it is language-specific. If you store an object or data structure from within Java into Couchbase Server, it will be serialized (transcoded) into a string that only the Java client library can understand. If you want to use the same information from a different client, you need to store it in a more generic format.

One of the more popular generic formats available is JSON. The popularity is based on a combination of its simplicity (it looks very similar to the nested hash structures of many scripting languages), and the fact that it can be used natively by JavaScript—and therefore within your web-based application—without any additional processing.

The JSON format is well described on the internet, and particularly at *http://json.org*. The best way to use JSON within Couchbase Server is to create and store your data by using the JSON hash structure to create an individual record. For example, you could define a basic beer record like this:

```
{
    "id": "beer_Hoptimus_Prime",
    "type": "beer",
    "abv": 10.0,
    "brewery": "Legacy Brewing Co.",
    "category": "North American Ale",
    "name": "Hoptimus Prime",
    "style": "Imperial or Double India Pale Ale",
}
```

The information is split into fields (for example, the brewery name), and types are implied by the JSON formatting as strings or floating point values.

Many languages include support for a similar hash, hashmap, or associative array structure, and there are libraries that will convert from an internal object into a JSON compatible format and back again.

 Looking forward to Couchbase Server 2.0 (which is already available in Developer Preview), using JSON when storing data will allow you to take advantage of the querying and indexing functionality. This works by parsing the stored documents in JSON format and picking out individual fields and other structures used to build a view into the data.

Expiry Times

We covered the role of expiry (or time to live [TTL]) times when looking at the core architecture of Couchbase Server. The expiry time is useful because it allows you to set a timeout on the information that you are storing so that it gets automatically deleted when it is no longer usable.

Other than using the `delete()` function, using the expiry value on a document is the only way to delete information from the database. Once the expiry time has been reached, the data will be deleted.

Expiration times are set either using a numeric value expressed as the number of seconds. For values less than 30 days (that is, 30*24*60*60 seconds), the value is taken as a relative value. For example, 3600 seconds would expire the document after one hour. For values higher than this, the value is interpreted as an absolute time expressed in seconds from the epoch.

Expiry can be useful in a number of different environments, but the most obvious is when using Couchbase Server to store session data for an application. You can set the expiry time to allow two hours of access to the website, with the session data being deleted when the user stops using the website for any period of time.

You can use the `touch()` and `getAndTouch()` functions to update the expiry while the user is still accessing the data, without having to explicitly set the expiry time through an update operation.

Flags

In addition to the expiry time, all documents are also stored with a set of flags. Not all client libraries expose the flags, but where they are available, you can use them to add information about a document, such as the document type.

Client Interaction with the Cluster

One of the most common questions when developing applications is how clients and client libraries react and are affected by the topology and topology changes that occur in a running cluster.

In general, a Couchbase Server cluster acts as a "black box" in terms of the client and database interaction. If you are using a smart client, the topology, node structure, and changes to this are entirely handled through the combination of the vBucket map and the client library.

The client library will take care of the communication between the client and the individual nodes. The node that you use to connect to the cluster when first opening a connection does not act as a proxy or distribution service.

Instead, a smart client (or Moxi) will load the vBucket map, and from this information, determine which node within the cluster should be contacted to store and retrieve different documents. The information exchange is direct with the right node for that data.

During a topology change (for example, a rebalance or failover operation), the client library should automatically handle any transient errors. In all other respects, the configuration and topology of the cluster is not something you should ever have to worry about.

CHAPTER 5

Monitoring Your Cluster

To fully understand how your cluster is working, and whether it is working effectively, there are a number of different statistics that you should monitor to diagnose and identify problems. Couchbase Server incorporates a huge range of statistics that provide very detailed and in-depth information on how your cluster is running.

Some of the statistics can be used on their own to provide advice and guidance; others may need to be monitored alongside other statistics to give a better picture. Others provide background information on how specific elements of your cluster are executing.

Monitoring Cluster, Nodes, Buckets

The architecture of Couchbase Server means that for the majority of statistics, you should monitor the cluster as a whole in the first instance.

Your monitoring should focus on:

Whole Cluster

Your whole cluster should be monitored to ensure that you are not running out of RAM, disk space, or I/O performance. A problem with any one of these items indicates that your cluster size should be increased.

You can monitor the overall performance from the main Cluster Overview page, shown in Figure 5-1.

Nodes

You should monitor your individual nodes to ensure that they are not experiencing spikes in CPU, RAM, or disk I/O. This may indicate that your cluster is failing to cope with RAM or I/O requirements, or that a node needs to be taken out of service (manual failover) due to a software or hardware issue.

You can monitor the key node statistics from the Server Nodes screen.

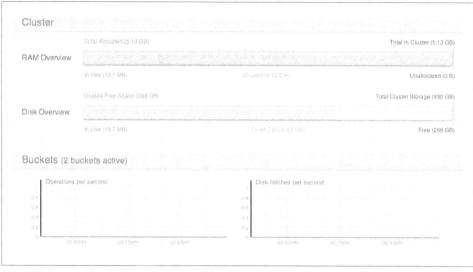

Figure 5-1. Cluster monitoring

Buckets

> Because of Couchbase Server's multitenancy model, it is possible to support multiple applications by using different buckets. You should monitor each of the configured buckets to determine if the problems in your cluster relate to a specific bucket. This will help you determine the best course of action, including adjusting the size of the bucket allocation on each node.
>
> You can monitor overall per-bucket statistics using the Monitor Data Buckets page within the Web console.

Monitoring RAM Usage

The overall RAM of your Couchbase Cluster is the most important aspect that you should monitor. Unlike many other databases, where all of the data is stored on disk and only cached in RAM, Couchbase stores the data in RAM, while persisting that information onto disk in the background. This distinction means that requests to read data come from memory first, and the disk second. Writing data to the cluster stores it in memory first, and ultimately writes it down to disk.

If the available RAM runs out, then Couchbase Server will start "ejecting" items from memory to make room for more active (i.e., more recently used) information. In a busy system, the effect is that more data is read from disk, and this has a cascade effect on disk write performance.

When monitoring RAM, you are therefore looking for overall RAM usage, cache-hit rates, and disk reads (which indicate that you are loading information from disk instead of providing the data from RAM). Through the statistics provided by Couchbase Server, you can also monitor the possible future impact of the current load by monitoring how items are being stored or ejected from memory.

The "watermark" determines when it is necessary to start freeing up available memory. Some important statistics related to watermarks are:

Low Watermark
> Replica data is ejected from memory once the memory level reaches this value.

High Watermark
> The system will start ejecting values out of memory when this watermark is met. Ejected values need to be fetched from disk when accessed, before being returned to the client.

If your system reaches the High Watermark, it may indicate that you are in danger of running out of RAM. You can monitor this overall (and the effect a lack of RAM is having) with the following statistics:

Memory Used
> The current size of memory used. If the memory used hits the RAM quota and no data can be ejected, you will get `OOM_ERROR`—that is, a generalized out of memory error. The `TMP_OOM` (or temporarily out of memory) error is returned when data still needs to be ejected but that hasn't happened yet. This means that the store or update operation failed, but the client should retry the operation again later.

Temp OOM errors per sec
> This should be 0. Any value higher than 0 indicates a lack of available memory, but of a transient nature. This may highlight a very busy cluster for a short period of time, unable to cope with the high level of traffic. You should continue to monitor the cluster overall to verify that it doesn't turn into a more permanent issue.

OOM errors per sec
> This should be 0. Any value higher than 0 this means that the cluster has run out of space to store information.

Cache Misses
> Ideally, this should be low. Increasing values mean that data your application expects to be available is not in memory.

If you notice problems in any of these statistics, then your cluster is in danger of running out of RAM. Couchbase Server will not stop operating and will continue to service requests, but the performance of the cluster will start to suffer. Expanding the cluster by adding more nodes will increase the available RAM and reduce this effect.

Monitoring Disk Usage

Couchbase Server persists information to disk. Failure to effectively persist the information to disk can have an effect on availability if a problem causes a failover scenario.

Disk Write Queue Size
> The size of the queue that has data waiting to be written to the disk. This value can be quite high in a busy cluster, but it should not increase over time because your cluster should be able to cope with the disk writes and request load.
>
> If the write queue is increasing, you need to improve the overall cluster I/O performance, which you can achieve by adding more nodes into your cluster. This distributes the disk I/O over more nodes, and therefore increases the overall cluster throughput.

Disk Fetches Per Second
> This parameter indicates how frequently Couchbase Server is having to go to disk in order to retrieve a request value, instead of serving the item from RAM. In a deployment where your entire data set is expected to fit in memory, this value should remain at zero.

Disk Utilization
> The overall disk space utilization, which is accessible on the Cluster Overview page, should be used to determine whether you are running out of physical disk space. You must have enough space to write the information that you are storing in the cluster down on to disk.

Monitoring Network Performance

The performance of your cluster is also affected by overall network performance and available network bandwidth. If you have too few servers, then you may reach either network utilization limits that further reduce the performance of your cluster.

Adding further nodes in this case will expand the available network bandwidth.

Monitoring within the Web Console

Statistics about the Couchbase Server cluster are shown according to the context of the section you are within. At the higher level, the statistics are shown at the cluster level, with the information aggregated across the cluster. For example, within the Cluster Overview page, the statistic information is shown for the whole cluster.

In addition to the aggregated information across the cluster, you can also drill down into more specific statistics at a bucket and/or server level of detail. The select mechanism for this information is common across the user interface.

Bucket Selection

The Data Buckets selection list allows you to select which of the buckets configured on your cluster is to be used as the basis for the graph display.

Server Selection

The Server Selection option enables you to select an individual server instead of viewing the aggregated cluster statistics. If you select an individual node, the console will display the Monitor: Server Nodes page within the Web Console for that note (see "Monitor: Server Nodes" on page 61). Selecting *All Server Nodes* shows the Monitor: Data Buckets page within the Web Console (see "Monitor: Data Buckets" on page 53).

Interval Selection

The Interval Selection option at the top of the main graph changes the interval display for all graphs displayed on the page. For example, selecting *Minute* shows information for the last minute, continuously updating.

 As the selected interval increases, the amount of statistical data displayed will change, depending on how long your cluster has been running.

Statistic Selection

All of the graphs within the display update simultaneously. Clicking on any of the smaller graphs will promote that graph to be displayed as the main graph for the page.

Aggregate Statistic By Server Selection

Clicking the blue triangle next to any of the smaller statistics graphs enables you to view the individual statistic across all the nodes within the cluster. This shows a single statistic, with individual graphs for each node in the cluster.

Monitor: Data Buckets

The *Data Buckets* list within the Monitor page displays a list of all the configured buckets on your system (of both Couchbase and Memcached types). The page provides a quick overview of your cluster health from the perspective of the configured buckets.

The information is shown in the form of a table, as seen in Figure 5-2.

Within the Monitor section for the list of available buckets, the information is displayed according to the bucket activity. The list of buckets is separated by the bucket type. For each bucket, the following information is provided in each column:

Couchbase Buckets				
Bucket Name	Ops/sec	Disk Fetches/sec	RAM Used	Item Count
contacts	0	0	23.3%	90009
default	0	0	10%	0
recipes	0	0	6.5%	0

Memcached Buckets				
Bucket Name	Ops/sec	Hit ratio	RAM Used	Item Count
webcache	0	0%	0%	0

Figure 5-2. Couchbase Web Console (Data Buckets overview)

Bucket Name
> The given name for the bucket. Clicking on the bucket name takes you to the individual bucket statistics page. For more information, see "Per-Bucket monitoring" on page 54.

Ops/sec
> Shows the number of operations per second for this data bucket.

Disk Fetches/sec
> Shows the number of read operations required to fetch items from disk.

RAM Used
> Shows the amount of RAM used against the configured bucket size.

Item Count
> Indicates the number of active objects stored in the bucket.

Per-Bucket monitoring

Selecting an individual bucket within the Couchbase Web Console displays detailed information about the per-bucket statistics. The following statistic groups are available for Couchbase bucket types.

Summary
> The summary section provides a quick overview of the cluster activity. For more information, see "Bucket monitoring (Summary statistics)" on page 55.

vBucket Resources
> This section provides detailed information on the vBucket resources across the cluster, including the active, replica, and pending operations. For more information, see "Bucket monitoring (vBucket Resources)" on page 56.

Disk Queues

Disk queues show the activity on the backend disk storage used for persistence within a data bucket. The information displayed shows the active, replica, and pending activity. For more information, see "Bucket monitoring (disk queues)" on page 57.

TAP Queues

The TAP queues section provides information on the activity within the TAP queues across replication, rebalancing, and client activity. For more information, see "Bucket monitoring (TAP queues)" on page 58.

Top Keys

This shows a list of the top 10 most actively used keys within the selected data bucket.

For Memcached bucket types, the Memcached static summary is provided. See "Bucket monitoring (Memcached buckets)" on page 60.

Bucket monitoring (Summary statistics)

The summary section is designed to provide a quick overview of the cluster activity. You can see an example of this in Figure 5-3. Each graph (or selected graph) shows information based on the currently selected bucket.

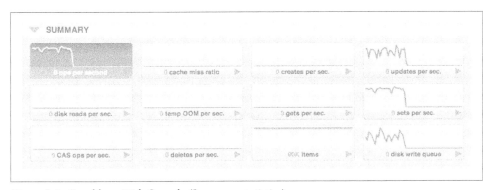

Figure 5-3. Couchbase Web Console (Summary statistics)

The following graph types are available:

ops per second

The total number of operations per second on this bucket.

cache miss ratio

Percentage of reads per second to this bucket that required a read from disk rather than RAM.

creates per sec.

Number of new items created in this bucket per second.

updates per sec.
> Number of existing items updated in this bucket per second.

disk reads per sec.
> Number of reads per second from disk for this bucket.

temp OOM per sec.
> Number of temporary out of memory errors sent per second to clients, due to out of memory situations for this bucket.

gets per sec.
> Number of client get operations per second for this bucket.

sets per sec.
> Number of client set operations per second for this bucket.

CAS ops per sec.
> Number of CAS (Compare and Swap) operations per second for this bucket.

deletes per sec.
> Number of client delete operations per second for this bucket.

items
> Number of items stored in this bucket.

disk write queue
> The size of the disk write queue used for persisting items down to disk.

Bucket monitoring (vBucket Resources)

The vBucket statistics, seen in Figure 5-4, provide information for all vBucket types within the cluster across three different states. Within the statistic display, the table of information is organized in four columns, showing the Active, Replica, and Pending states for each individual statistic. The final column provides the total value for each statistic.

The Active column displays the information for vBuckets within the Active state. The Replica column displays the statistics for vBuckets within the Replica state (i.e., currently being replicated). The Pending column shows statistics for vBuckets in the Pending state (i.e., while data is being exchanged during rebalancing).

These states are shared across all the following statistics. For example, the graph *new items per sec* within the Active state column displays the number of new items per second created within the vBuckets that are in the active state.

The individual statistics, one for each state, shown are:

vBuckets
> The number of vBuckets within the specified state.

items
> Number of items within the vBucket of the specified state.

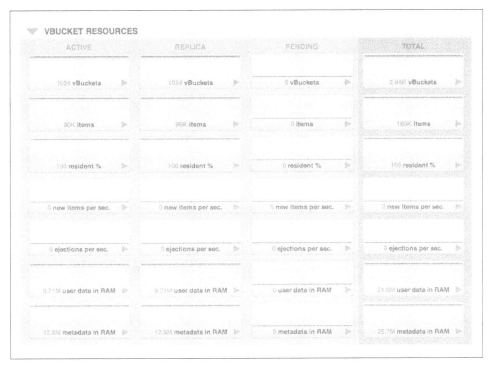

Figure 5-4. Couchbase Web Console (vBucket Resources statistics)

resident %
> Percentage of items within the vBuckets of the specified state that are resident (in RAM).

new items per sec.
> Number of new items created in vBuckets within the specified state.

ejections per sec.
> Number of items ejected per second within the vBuckets of the specified state.

user data in RAM
> Size of user data within vBuckets of the specified state that are resident in RAM.

metadata in RAM
> Size of item metadata within the vBuckets of the specified state that are resident in RAM.

Bucket monitoring (disk queues)

The Disk Queues statistics section displays the information for data being placed into the disk queue (see Figure 5-5). Disk queues are used within Couchbase Server to store the information written to disk for persistence. Information is displayed for each of the disk queues corresponding to the vBuckets in their respective states, Active, Replica, and Pending, with the aggregate of these operations provided in the last column.

Figure 5-5. Couchbase Web Console (Disk Queue statistics)

The Active column displays the information for the Disk Queues for the vBuckets within the Active state. The Replica column displays the statistics for the Disk Queues with vBuckets in the Replica state (i.e., currently being replicated). The Pending column shows statistics for the Disk Queues for vBuckets in the Pending state (i.e., while data is being exchanged during rebalancing).

These states are shared across all the following statistics. For example, the graph *fill rate* within the Replica state column displays the number of items being put into the replica disk queue for the selected bucket.

The displayed statistics are:

items
> The number of items waiting to be written to disk for this bucket for this state.

fill rate
> The number of items per second being added to the disk queue for the corresponding state.

drain rate
> Number of items per second written to disk from the disk queue for the corresponding state.

average age
> The average age of items (in seconds) within the disk queue for the specified state.

Bucket monitoring (TAP queues)

The TAP queues statistics are designed to show information about the TAP queue activity between cluster nodes and clients. The statistics information is therefore organized as a table, with columns showing the statistics for TAP queues used for replication, rebalancing, and clients (see Figure 5-6). An aggregate of these values is provided in the final column.

Figure 5-6. Couchbase Web Console (TAP Queues statistics)

The statistics in this section are detailed below:

TAP senders
> Number of TAP queues in this bucket for rebalancing or client connections.

items
> Number of items waiting to be sent in the corresponding TAP queue for this bucket.

drain rate
> Number of items per second being sent over the corresponding TAP queue connections to this bucket.

back-off rate
> Number of back-offs per second sent when sending data through the corresponding TAP connection to this bucket.

backfill remaining
> Number of items in the backfill queue for the corresponding TAP connection for this bucket.

remaining on disk
> Number of items still on disk that need to be loaded to service the TAP connection to this bucket.

Bucket monitoring (Memcached buckets)

For Memcached buckets, a separate suite of memcached-specific statistics are displayed (see Figure 5-7).

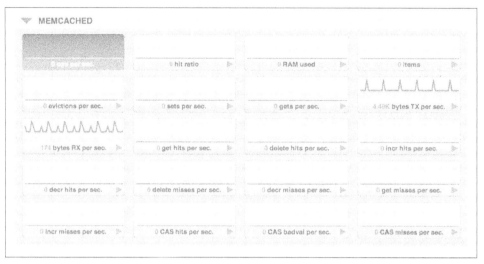

Figure 5-7. Couchbase Web Console (Memcached statistics)

The Memcached statistics are:

ops per sec.
    Total operations per second serviced by this bucket.

hit ratio
    Percentage of get requests served with data from this bucket.

RAM used
    Total amount of RAM used by this bucket.

items
    Number of items stored in this bucket.

evictions per sec.
    Number of items per second evicted from this bucket.

sets per sec.
    Number of set operations serviced by this bucket.

gets per sec.
    Number of get operations serviced by this bucket.

bytes TX per sec.
    Number of bytes per second sent from this bucket.

bytes RX per sec.
  Number of bytes per second sent into this bucket.

get hits per sec.
  Number of get operations per second for data that this bucket contains.

delete hits per sec.
  Number of delete operations per second for data that this bucket contains.

incr hits per sec.
  Number of increment operations per second for data that this bucket contains.

decr hits per sec.
  Number of decrement operations per second for data that this bucket contains.

delete misses per sec.
  Number of delete operations per second for data that this bucket does not contain.

decr misses per sec.
  Number of decr operations per second for data that this bucket does not contain.

get Misses per sec.
  Number of get operations per second for data that this bucket does not contain.

incr misses per sec.
  Number of increment operations per second for data that this bucket does not contain.

CAS hits per sec.
  Number of CAS operations per second for data that this bucket contains.

CAS badval per sec.
  Number of CAS operations per second using an incorrect CAS ID for data that this bucket contains.

CAS misses per sec.
  Number of CAS operations per second for data that this bucket does not contain.

Monitor: Server Nodes

In addition to monitoring buckets over all the nodes within the cluster, Couchbase Server also includes support for monitoring the statistics for an individual node.

The Server Nodes monitoring overview (see Figure 5-8) shows summary data for the Swap Usage, RAM Usage, CPU Usage, and Active Items across all the nodes in your cluster.

Selecting a server from the list shows a server-specific version of the Bucket Monitoring overview, showing a combination of the server-specific performance information, and the overall statistic information for the bucket across all nodes. You can see an example of this in Figure 5-9.

Figure 5-8. Couchbase Web Console (Server Nodes overview)

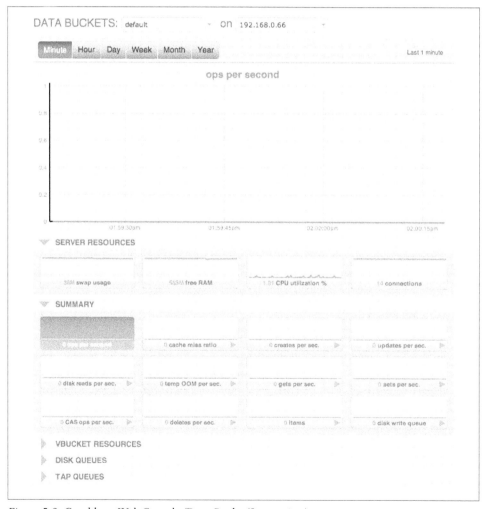

Figure 5-9. Couchbase Web Console (Data Bucket/Server view)

The graphs specific to the server are:

swap usage
Amount of swap space in use on this server.

free RAM
Amount of RAM available on this server.

CPU utilization %
Percentage of CPU utilized across all cores on the selected server.

connections
Number of connects to this server of all types for client, proxy, TAP requests, and internal statistics.

You can select an individual bucket and server to view a statistic using the pop-up selections for the server and bucket, and clicking on the mini-graph for a given statistic, as shown in Figure 5-10.

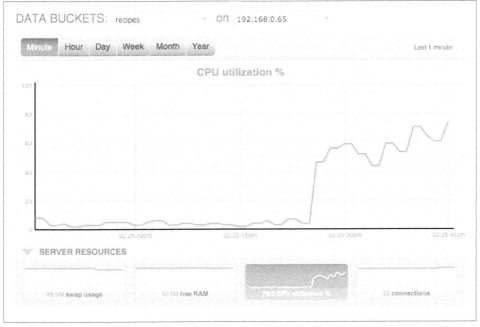

Figure 5-10. Couchbase Web Console (Server-specific view)

For more information on the data bucket statistics, see the section "Monitor: Data Buckets" on page 53.

CHAPTER 6

Managing Your Cluster

Couchbase Server is largely self-managing. There are few configuration variables, and most of these do not need to be modified by most users. You also do not need to perform regular maintenance to your cluster or data. Couchbase automatically manages this as part of the standard operation.

The result is that management of your cluster is only required when human intervention of some kind is required, for example:

Expanding or shrinking your cluster
> As you store information in your cluster and the load on your cluster increases or requires more data storage, you will need to increase the size of your cluster. The converse may also be true. For example, if you have deployed your application within a cloud service such as Amazon EC2, you will want to shrink the size of your cluster when the RAM or disk I/O requirements recede to lower your running costs.
>
> The act of expanding and shrinking your cluster is called rebalancing and can be performed on a live, running cluster.

Handle a failover
> If a note within your cluster fails for some reason (hardware or network failure are the most common), then Couchbase Server can switch to one of the replicas of the data. Failover can be manual or automatic, and there are different considerations for the two methods, which are both described later in this chapter.

Backing up and/or restoring your data
> Although Couchbase Server automatically distributes your data, and creates 1-3 replicas of your bucket data, it is good practice to back up and restore your data in the event of a failure. Backup and restore is covered in "Backup and Restore" on page 71.

Let's take a closer look at each of these key management tasks.

Expanding and Shrinking Your Cluster (Rebalancing)

Over the lifetime of your Couchbase cluster, there will very likely be cause to add or remove nodes. This can be based upon a variety of factors including RAM/disk capacity and available network bandwidth, as well as the need for maintenance such as upgrades. The process of adding or removing nodes from your Couchbase cluster consists of a rebalancing process, which at its core, is meant to evenly distribute data across the cluster while providing continuous availability of data.

The rebalancing process performs the following operations, all while the cluster remains up and running:

- Moves data within the vBuckets from the existing node structure to the new node structure. The process is the same whether you are adding or removing nodes, and the purpose is to ensure that the vBucket allocation matches the new cluster structure.

- While the data is being moved, existing client requests continue to read and write information based on the current node structure. Any updates to the data are recorded and transferred over to the new structure.

- The updated layout and distribution of the vBuckets across the cluster is updated incrementally as each vBucket is moved. The updated structure replaces the old structure, and smart clients and the Moxi service are updated with the new information. From this point on, all requests will go to the new nodes as determined by the updated structure.

The rebalancing process therefore allows the cluster to continue operating as normal even while the structure and number of the nodes is being modified. Obviously, the time taken to adjust the node configuration depends entirely on the amount of data in your cluster, and how many nodes are being added or removed as well as load.

The same process can be used to perform software upgrades and hardware refreshes by removing a node, making changes and then rebalancing it back into the cluster. If possible, for these operations it is a best practice to add the additional nodes first before removing nodes.

All changes to the cluster, whether shrinking or growing, are a two-phase process. First, you must add or remove the node or nodes from the existing structure. Then, you must rebalance the cluster to move the data around and reconfigure the cluster structure.

Once you decide to add or remove nodes to your Couchbase cluster, there are a few things to take into consideration:

- If you're planning on adding and/or removing multiple nodes in a short period of time, it is best to add them all at once and then kick off the rebalancing operation rather than rebalance after each addition. This will reduce the overall load placed on the system as well as the amount of data that needs to be moved.

- Choose a quiet time for adding nodes. While the rebalancing operation is meant to be performed online, it is not a "free" operation and will put increased load on the system as a whole in the form of disk IO, network bandwidth, CPU resources, and RAM usage.
- It is our recommended best practice to do any "voluntary" (i.e., not to resolve a failure) rebalancing operation during a period of low usage of the system. Obviously with today's 24/7 web applications, there may not be a period of complete inactivity, but it is up to the administrator to understand the impact that a rebalancing operation may have on the cluster and application.
- Memory required for rebalancing. The rebalancing operation requires moving large amounts of data around the cluster. The more RAM that is available, the more disk access your operating system can cache, which will allow it to perform the rebalancing operation much faster. If there is not enough memory in your cluster, the rebalancing may be quite slow. In general, you should avoid waiting for your cluster to reach full capacity before adding more capacity and then rebalancing.

Adding a Node

Choosing when to add a node is usually based on clear evidence provided from the statistics that show either you are running out of RAM, disk space, disk I/O, or network performance.

You can add a node to an existing cluster using two different methods: either during the initial installation when first installing Couchbase Server, or if Couchbase Server has already been installed, by adding the node from within the existing cluster.

During the Setup phase when configuring a new node for the first time, you can opt to join an existing cluster. To add the new node to an existing cluster, enter the IP address of any node within the current cluster, as well as the administrator username and password.

Alternatively, if the node is already up and running, and Couchbase Server is already running on the node, you can add it from the existing cluster. To do this within the Web console, switch to the Manage→Server Nodes page within the Web Console and click the Add Server button. You will be presented with a dialog box (see Figure 6-1) where you must specify the IP address of the new node, and the administrator username and password of the Couchbase server being added to the new cluster.

If you use this method, any data on that node (even if it was running as a separate cluster) will be removed in preparation for a rebalance in this cluster.

You can repeat this as many times as you need for the number of nodes that you want to add to the system.

Regardless of the method you choose, the Web Console should show that you have one or more machines that require a rebalance.

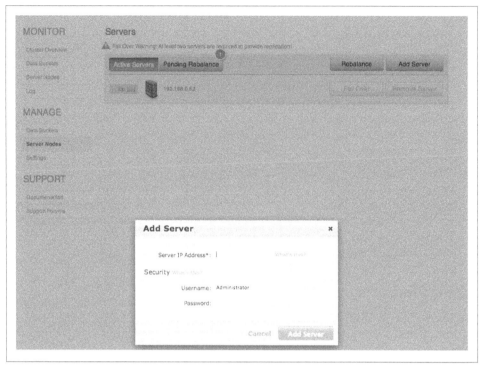

Figure 6-1. Adding an existing node

Removing a Node

Choosing to shrink a Couchbase cluster is a more subjective decision. It is usually based upon cost considerations and/or not needing as large a cluster to support the load requirements of your application.

When deciding to shrink a cluster, it is important to ensure you have enough capacity in the remaining nodes to support your dataset as well as your application load.

Removing multiple nodes at once is not recommended, because the effect on the load and capacity of your cluster could be significant. Although the statistics may indicate that you can remove a node due to excess RAM or I/O, removing multiple nodes in one operation may significantly increase other statistics that affect overall performance. Removing the nodes one at a time will enable you to monitor the effects without such a dramatic effect on the cluster performance.

To remove a server from the cluster, go to the Server Nodes management screen and click the Remove Server button. You will be asked to confirm the removal. Once confirmed, the server is only marked for removal from the cluster. The actual removal process only takes place during the rebalance operation. You must wait until the rebalance operation has completed before disabling or switching off the node in question.

It is recommended that you remove a node rather than fail it over. When a node fails and is not coming back to the cluster, the failover functionality will promote its replica vBuckets to become active immediately. If a healthy node is failed over, there might be some data loss for the replication data that was in flight during that operation. Using the remove functionality will ensure that all data is properly replicated and continuously available.

Rebalancing

To perform a rebalance, go to the Server Nodes management page and click the Rebalance button. This will start the rebalance process, as shown in Figure 6-2.

 The exact time taken from this process will depend on the size of your cluster, the number of existing nodes, how busy the cluster is, and how nodes are included in the rebalance operation.

Figure 6-2. Rebalancing

The Web Console will allow you to monitor the process so that you can determine how much work is left and when the process has been successfully completed.

Failover with Couchbase

In Couchbase Server, failing over a server (and thus, transferring load to replica servers for the document IDs that were previously "active" on that server) can be done either manually, automatically, or programmatically.

Failover within Couchbase is the process that immediately activates any replica vBuckets for the vBuckets that were active on the node being failed over.

Ideally, you should only fail over a node that is down, and also only if you know you have replicas available elsewhere in the cluster.

If a node is not down, you should attempt to use the remove/rebalance functionality, as this will ensure all the data is removed, re-replicated and maintained safely. See "Rebalancing" on page 69. Failing over a live node may introduce a small data-loss window, as any data "in flight" (meaning not yet replicated) will be lost when the failover takes place.

 Failover is a comparatively passive operation. Failover doesn't recreate or copy any data—instead, it just activates the already generated replicas of the vBuckets that were created when the data was written to the cluster. Failover updates the vBucket map so that vBuckets that were previously replicas of the original data are now the active vBuckets.

Automatic Failover

Automatic Failover allows Couchbase Server to monitor the nodes and automatically switch to a replica if it identifies a problem.

There are issues with this model, in that the problem may be transient or unknown, the system can failover a node that didn't need to be failed over, or there will be a problem when there are no more spare replicas.

- Automatic failover is off by default. Best practice would be to have an external system (either human or automated) monitoring the Couchbase cluster to prevent other external factors from causing additional problems..
- If multiple nodes go down simultaneously, then automatic failover will not be triggered, even if it has been enabled.
- Automatic failover is only available on clusters of at least three nodes.
- The Automatic failover feature will only fail over one node before requiring administrative interaction. This is to prevent a cascading failure from taking the cluster completely out of operation.

There is a minimum 30 second delay before a node will be automatically failed over. This can be raised, but the software is hardcoded to perform multiple "pings" of a node that is perceived to be down. This is to prevent a slow node or flaky network connection from being failed-over inappropriately.

If there are any node failures, an email can be configured to be sent out both when an automatic failover occurs, and when it doesn't.

Resetting the Auto failover counter

After a node has been automatically failed over, the administrator must reset the counter in order for the autofailover feature to work again.

This should only be done after restoring the cluster to a healthy and balanced state.

Monitored Failover

Whether you chose to use automatic failover or manual failover, the best solution is to use monitoring to drive the failover decision. Monitored failover using manual intervention can take two forms: human or external system.

Human intervention

One option is to have a human operator respond to alerts and make a decision on what to do. Humans are uniquely capable of considering a wide range of data, observations, and experience to best resolve a situation. Many organizations disallow automated failover without human consideration of the implications. But that's not always a feasible solution for companies (large or small).

External monitoring

Another option is to have a system monitoring the cluster via the Management REST API. Such an external system is in the best position to order the failover of nodes, because it can take into account system components that are outside the scope of Couchbase visibility. For example, by observing that a network switch is flaking and that there is a dependency on that switch by the Couchbase cluster, the management system may determine that failing the Couchbase nodes will not help the situation.

If, however, everything around Couchbase and across the various nodes is healthy, it does indeed look like a single node problem, and the aggregate traffic can support loading the remaining nodes with all traffic, then the management system may fail the system over. Couchbase fully supports this model through its REST interface.

Backup and Restore

Backing up your data should be a regular process on your cluster to ensure that you do not lose information in the event of a serious hardware or installation failure.

The recommended method for performing a backup is to use the cbbackup command.

This method saves the data store in the cluster in a format that does not take into account the cluster topology. You can use this method on a running cluster without disabling or shutting the cluster while it is still running.

You can use this method to restore to a completely different cluster, with a different configuration, topology, and hardware environment.

For detailed instructions, see "Backup" on page 72. For detailed information on the restore processes and options, see "Restore" on page 73.

 It is a best practice to back up and restore all nodes together to minimize any inconsistencies in data. Couchbase is always per-item consistent, but does not guarantee total cluster consistency or in-order persistence.

Backup

You can take a backup of a running Couchbase node. The `cbbackup` script copies the data in the data files, but the backup process must be performed on each bucket and on all nodes of a cluster to take a backup of that cluster. The command does not back up all the data automatically.

The `cbbackup` script takes the following arguments:

```
cbbackup [bucket_path_name] [dest_dir_path].
```

Make sure that there is enough disk space to take the backup.

> The user running the `cbbackup` command must have the correct permissions to read/write to the files being backed up, and run the necessary additional commands that are executed during the process.
>
> Recommended best practice is to run the command as the `couchbase` user, as this is the default owner of the files when Couchbase Server is installed.

The `cbbackup` script will also perform a *vacuum* of the database files to defragment them, which provides faster startup times. Depending on the amount of data, this script can take an extended amount of time to run. It is a best practice to make sure that your connection to the server running the script is not broken.

Linux

Open Powershell and run the following backup:

```
shell> cbbackup /opt/couchbase/var/lib/couchbase/data/default-data /backups/
2010-12-22/
```

Back up the configuration file located at */opt/couchbase/var/lib/couchbase/config/config.dat*.

Windows

Open Powershell. Set the execution policy for the session:

```
shell> set-executionpolicy remotesigned
```

Run the backup on the specified bucket:

```
shell> cbbackup "C:\Program Files\Couchbase\Server\var\lib\couchbase\data
\default-data" \
    "C:/backup/2010-12-22/"
```

Copy the *config.dat* file, located at *C:\Program Files\Couchbase\Server\var\lib\couchbase\config\config.dat*.

Restore

When restoring a backup, you have to select the appropriate restore sequence based on the type of restore you are performing. There are a number of methods of restoring your cluster:

Restoring a cluster to a previous state, to the same cluster
> This method should be used when you are restoring information to an identical cluster, or directly back to the cluster from which the backup was made. The cluster will need to be identically configured, with the same number of nodes and identical IP addresses to the cluster at the point when it was backed up.
>
> For advice on using this method, see the section "Restoring to the same cluster" on page 73.

Restoring a cluster to a previous state, to a different cluster
> If your cluster environment has changed in any way (for example, changes to the hardware or underlying configuration, such as disk layout or IP addresses), then you should use this method. When using Couchbase Server within a virtual or cloud environment, the IP address and/or size configuration is likely to have changed considerably. The number of nodes in the cluster should be identical.
>
> For advice on using this method, see the section "Restoring to a different cluster" on page 74.

Restoring a cluster to a different configuration
> If you want to restore data to a cluster with a different configuration, or in the event of a corruption of your existing cluster data, then you can use the cbrestore tool. This natively restores data back into a new cluster and new configuration.
>
> For advice on using this method, see the section "Restoring using cbrestore tool" on page 75.

 Make sure that any restoration of files also sets the proper ownership of those files to the couchbase user

Restoring to the same cluster

To restore the information to the same cluster, with the same configuration, you must shut down your entire cluster while you restore the data, and then restart the cluster again. You are replacing the entire cluster data and configuration with the backed up version of the data files, and then restarting the cluster with the saved version of the cluster files.

When restoring data back in to the same cluster, then the following must be true before proceeding:

- The cluster must contain the same number of nodes.
- Each node must have the IP address or hostname it was configured with when the cluster was backed up.
- You must restore all of the *config.dat* configuration files, as well as all of the database files to their original locations.

The steps required to complete the restore process are:

1. Stop the Couchbase Server service on all nodes.
2. On each node, restore the database and configuration files from your backup copies for each node.
3. Restart the service on each node.

Restoring to a different cluster

To restore the data to a different cluster, you take a backup of the data, and recreate the bucket configuration on a new cluster. This enables Couchbase Server to load the data into the new cluster and repopulate the database with the backed up data. You cannot change the topology or number of nodes within the cluster using this method, but you can modify the physical characteristics of each node, including the hardware configuration or IP addresses.

You can use this feature to migrate an entire cluster into a new set of machines. This is particularly useful:

- In cloud environments, where the IP addresses of nodes will have changed
- When hardware configuration, such as RAM size, disk hardware, or disk configuration and/or environment has changed.
- To create dev/test clusters with the same data as the production cluster

To restore a cluster using this method, the following must be true:

- You have a backup of each of the buckets in your cluster made using the cbbackup command.
- The two clusters must have the same number of nodes.
- The original cluster must be in a healthy state. This means that all nodes should be up and running and no rebalance or failover operation should be running.
- It is a best practice for both clusters to be of the same OS and memory configuration.

The necessary steps for migrating data using this method are as follows:

1. Take a backup of the data files of all nodes, using the above procedure. Alternately, shut down the couchbase-server on all nodes and copy the DB files.
2. Install Couchbase Server (of at least version 1.7.1) on new nodes and cluster together. If using the web console to setup your cluster, a "default" bucket will be created. Please delete this bucket before proceeding.
3. Place the copies of the original files into the data directory on all the new nodes.

 You do not have to "match" up the nodes one-for-one. However, ensure that each set of original data files gets placed onto one and only one node of the new cluster

 Please ensure that you retain file ownership properties for those files which you placed on the destination node.

4. Start couchbase-server on the new nodes.
5. Create a bucket with the same name and SASL configuration on the new nodes.
6. After the bucket creation, each node will start loading items from the data files into memory.
7. The cluster will be in a balanced state after warm up.
8. Do not start a rebalance process while nodes are still warming up.
9. If any nodes go down during the warmup, it is a best practice to restart all nodes together.

Restoring using cbrestore tool

This is useful if:

- You want to restore data into a cluster of a different size
- You want to transfer/restore data into a different bucket

The cbrestore tool provides the following options:

```
Usage: cbrestore [opts] db_files (use -h for detailed help)

Options:
  -h, --help            show this help message and exit
  -a, --add             Use add instead of set to avoid overwriting existing
                        items
  -H HOST, --host=HOST  Hostname of moxi server to connect to
  -p PORT, --port=PORT  Port of moxi server to connect to
  -u USERNAME, --username=USERNAME
                        Bucket username (usually the bucket name) to
                        authenticate to moxi with
  -P PASSWORD, --password=PASSWORD
                        Bucket password to authenticate to moxi with
```

```
 -t THREADS, --threads=THREADS
                        Number of worker threads
 -k KEY, --key=KEY      Keys to restore which match regular expression
 -d DATA, --data=DATA   Server side value to match
 -i ID, --id=ID         vbucketID to restore
 -v, --verbose          verbose logging
```

```
Restore keys from the sqlite backing store files from a single node.
```

Depending on the amount of data, this script can take an extended amount of time to run. It is a best practice to make sure that your connection to the server running the script is not broken, or that you are using something to let the script run in the background (i.e., screen):

```
shell> cbrestore -a default default-0.mb default-1.mb default-2.mb default-3.mb
```

In order to correctly restore, you must put all of the database backup file names as command arguments:

```
shell> cd "C:/Program Files/Couchbase/Server/bin/"
shell> cbrestore -a "C:/backup/2010-12-22/default" "C:/backup/2010-12-22/
default-0.mb" \
    "C:/backup/2010-12-22/default-1.mb" "C:/backup/2010-12-22/default-2.mb" "C:/
backup/2010-12-22/default-3.mb"
```

About the Author

A professional writer for over 15 years, Martin "MC" Brown is the author and contributor to over 26 books covering an array of topics, including programming, system management, and web technologies. His expertise spans myriad development languages and platforms—Perl, Python, Java, JavaScript, Basic, Pascal, Modula-2, C, C++, Rebol, Gawk, Shellscript, Windows, Solaris, Linux, BeOS, Microsoft WP, Mac OS, and more. The combination has resulted in expertise in web programming, systems management and integration, and XML and DocBook technologies for writing and publishing documentation.

MC is a former LAMP Technologies Editor for *LinuxWorld* magazine and a regular contributor to ServerWatch.com, LinuxPlanet, ComputerWorld, and IBM developerWorks. As a Subject Matter Expert for Microsoft, he provided technical input to their Windows Server and certification teams. He draws on a rich and varied background as a founding member of a leading UK ISP, systems manager and IT consultant for an advertising agency and Internet solutions group, technical specialist for an intercontinental ISP network, and database designer and programmer—and as a self-confessed compulsive consumer of computing hardware and software. In his pre-writing life, he spent more than 10 years designing and managing mixed platform environments. As a result, he has developed a rare talent of being able to convey the benefits and intricacies of his subject with equal measures of enthusiasm, professionalism, in-depth knowledge, and insight.

A past technical writer building both the documentation system and writing content for MySQL and the MySQL groups within Sun and then Oracle, MC is currently the VP of Technical Publications and Education for Couchbase and is responsible for all published documentation, training programs, and content.

Have it your way.